A TREK THROUGH THE TAPESTRY OF TIME

JAISON CHACKO

Dedicated to two sweet people: my granddaughters, Maria and Serah, who came into my life very late, but filled up the empty space in my heart that I never knew I had.

They brought more love, joy and affection and made my current world softer and warmer.

Dear Appappa's sweet girls, carve out your own paths in life with courage and kindness!

CONTENTS

FOREWORD

"The invariable mark of wisdom is to see the miraculous in the common."

– Ralph Waldo Emerson, American Essayist.

It was in 1984 that Jaison Chacko and I arrived in Qatar, a small country with a population of just about one of India's 543 parliamentary constituencies, to join Albalagh, a contracting firm. Qatar and Albalagh were relatively unknown. Many times, while introducing ourselves, we had to spell out these words and locate Qatar for them on a map. All that is in the past.

Buoyed by an oil-rich economy and a stable government, Qatar, the 'Little Giant,' was already stirring and was on the cusp of riding the crest of prosperity. Today, Qatar is the richest country in terms of per capita income. The successful conduct of the 2022 football World Cup, a challenge and a dare for even some of the leading industrialized nations, added to the statute of Qatar among nations.

During the 30 years that Jaison Chacko was here with Albalagh, until his retirement in 2014, mostly at the helm of affairs, Albalagh was transformed from a small contracting company to one of Qatar's reputable, diversified, and respected companies. Albalagh has also played its part in shaping Qatar's world-class infrastructure, expanding landscape, and the ever-changing skyline of Doha, the capital city. In the year 2013, as a jewel in the crown, Albalagh was awarded the title of 'The Best National Company' in Qatar.

The writer in Jaison was probably always there. It must have been his hectic career as a corporate head in a challenging multinational environment that delayed its emergence. His professional experience travels across the world, interest in reading, and keen observation skills were all subconsciously at work and dormant, moulding the writer in him. As in nature, there is a time in one's life when there is a trigger which releases the passion that builds up within. In Jaison's case, it was the demise of his brother 'Thavo', who was three years older than him, with whom he shared an intense and profound relationship both as a brother and as a friend, that awoke the writer in him. "Adios, Chettan" was the first. It's an imaginary email he sent to his brother informing him of the eventful two days when his body was in the wake at his family home before the final rites.

"Adios……. Chettan" in October 2011, marked the beginning of the writer and essayist Jaison Chacko and also of the blog "Musings from Doha." An article a month on the first of every month, like clockwork, a practice that is still continuing and a highlight of this blog. Many times, it's only when I receive the link to this blog by WhatsApp that I realize it's the first of the month, and I am reminded of the bills to settle. His determination and commitment to his readers in adhering to this timeline are awesome. Over the years, this blog has caught the imagination of a small community all across the world, with readers from over 110 countries and over 400K plus views and counting. I am honoured and privileged to forward this third book, *A Trek Through The Tapestry of Time*, the sequel to "Gandhi? Who is That?" and "Kaleidoscopic Musings," a collection of the author's selected articles covering a wide range of topics. A cursory glance through the "Table of Contents" will reveal the diversity of topics. This collection of articles with eye-catching titles will live up to your expectations as they delve into the intriguing and often overlooked yet relevant aspects of the subject. These topics are hand-picked with care, judiciously and after a lot of research. Yet another highlight of this blog.

In addition to the articles that are published on the first of every month, there is the occasional bonus like "Mohawk! Acrophiles of New York City" in this edition, a tribute to Sri N. Govindankutty on his

demise, a friend for over 50 years. In this article, we are introduced to the Mohawks, known as 'Skywalkers', who belong to an indigenous American tribe. Acrophiles who work on steel girders at dizzying heights, defying gravity, and have made possible some of America's iconic skyscrapers of a period, including the Empire State Building.

The author's articles in his field of experience, corporate management, contracts, and career are not necessarily approached from a textbook perspective but rather from his personal experiences and, at times, a street-smart approach to resolving even complex issues. In "Be Sure to Put Your Feet in the Right Place – Then Stand Firm," a career tip to youngsters, the life of Abraham Lincoln is taken as an example. Little-known facts about Abraham Lincoln's early life, from being a barman to a professional wrestler, among others, until he finally found his calling, at which point he put his feet down, stood firm, and went on to become one of America's most loved and admired presidents.

As you delve through the pages of this book, you will find that every article is, in a way, unique and with an element of surprise. You probably would not have heard of Oshiya in "Oshiya – Professional Pushers of Tokyo Metro!" nor about the origin or value of ambergris in "Ambergris – Floating Treasures of the Sea". You would not have heard of Dr William Hamilton or his role in the rise of the East India Company in India in "From the Diary of a British Surgeon Who Made Passage to India Easier". Could you have imagined that Pepsi was once a naval power? The article "Pepsi: How They Once Owned the Sixth Largest Fleet in the World" reveals it all.

"Maria and Serah.... Mary Had a Little Lamb!" is a tribute by a doting grandfather to his loving grandchildren. The story, the myth, and the controversies surrounding the ever-so-popular nursery rhyme are worth reading.

If the subject of the article is from one of the author's many travels, it will not be about any major tourist attraction of the place, but rather something that you would have missed while travelling and probably regret now. In "Dolmen of Marayoor," the author brings to the attention of the authorities the dilapidated state of these structures in Kerala, his home state in India. I am also a witness to this state of neglect. Dolmens (prehistoric burial sites) are not confined to Kerala or India. They are found in many countries, mostly protected and are tourist attractions. Dolmen in Korea are even protected as UNESCO heritage sites.

Titanic is a shipwreck that has shocked the world. In "Man Makes Plans, God Laughs," the author tells the story of another shipwreck, "The Wreck of the Titan," a novel written by Morgan Robertson 14 years before the Titanic. The article goes on to reveal some of the striking similarities between the two accidents. The book and the author became a runaway success following the Titanic.

In the article "Master Shipbuilders of India Crafted World Class Warships for Royal British Navy", we become aware of a thriving shipbuilding industry and master craftsmen who, during the British colonial rule, supplied hundreds of ships by order to the British Navy and the Merchant Navy. The role played by Jamsetjee Bomanjee of Wadia Shipbuilders, along with seven generations of the Wadia family, in supplying the Royal Navy with world-class warships, including the HMS Minden, HMS Trincomalee, and HMS Cornwallis, is well documented. We also come to know of the role the Indian shipbuilding industry has contributed in supporting the Royal Navy to reign supreme over the high seas. In the article "Heavenly Fragrance of Gods was from India," we are reminded, but not known to many, of India's domination in the perfume and fragrance industry as early as 1400 BC, along with historical references in support of this. The exotic perfume derived from Oud, the resin of Agarwood wood popularly known as the "Fragrance of the Gods," has its origins in India. After reading these two articles, the staunch nationalist in the author leaves us thinking as to why such accomplishments did not find due mention by historians or as to why they don't find a place in textbooks for a new generation to grow up proud of their history, traditions, and achievements.

In this enchanting realm of curiosity and knowledge, this collection of articles will embark you on an odyssey that will ignite your intellect and kindle the flames of wonder. *A Trek Through The Tapestry of Time* should find its rightful place in your home library for your family and friends and also for you to revisit and relive the experience you once had. These articles have been so thoughtfully selected; they will always be a delight to read, as these nuggets of knowledge can transcend time.

– JOMY JOSEPH

EXECUTIVE ENGINEER(RETD)
KERALA STATE IRRIGATION DEPT.

ACKNOWLEDGEMENTS

This is my third book published; all the articles featured were written during the last two years – since 2022 – enjoying my retired life in Kochi, India. More than anything else, hours of research and positiveness kept my mind busy as ever. It helped flow of blood into my head – at least 30 hours – from inception to completion of each article.

I thank my immediate family members, Vinay, Vishal, and Anu, for all the support they gave me. In fact, the presence of two granddaughters – Maria and Serah – who used to spend weekends with us along with their parents always gave Geetha and me something to look forward to in my current life. They have influenced me for sure in writing and publishing my third book a reality. They have unknowingly pushed me to some other roles also – a performing Magician and a Quizmaster! While we sat together around the dining table for breakfast on Sundays, I used to get questions prepared and ready on various topics, including my favourite of theirs: space and oceanography. These moments were all epitomes of happiness for me at this stage and age of life.

Special thanks to Mr. Jomy Joseph, who gave consent to write a Foreword, which has come out nice with his impeccable English. Please read it if you have not already. I thank Geetha, my wife, who has been proofreading the drafts of all my articles. I also thank Google for permitting me to make use of some of the images in the book. My blog is www.jaisonchacko.com, and my email is chackojaison@hotmail.com.

– JAISON CHACKO

PUTHOOR
#3, GEORGE EDEN Road,
Kochi-6820217.

MARIA AND SERAH... MARY HAD A LITTLE LAMB!

Some of the best moments I have had in my retired life, after settling in my hometown 8 years ago, have been the times spent with my grandchildren. Nothing unusual compared to what the world generally experiences, but still, I consider myself lucky. These moments are filled with love and happiness, light-hearted laughter, and much more that only such grandparents and grandchildren can fully understand! It is said that genes skip a generation, though I don't know whether this is scientifically true. Perhaps that's why grandparents find their grandchildren so likeable!

One thing I've been reintroduced to during this period is nursery rhymes, which my grandchildren went through while attending play schools. To the best of my understanding, a nursery rhyme in English or any language is a poem or song revolving around certain traditions or folklore. They are rhythmic and intended to amuse young children. Such rhymes are always imaginary and have nothing to do with actual events, though they have been passed down through generations for centuries.

However, I recently learned that at least one among the hundreds of old nursery rhymes is based on an actual event. That's to do with Mary and her lamb. There was indeed a Mary who lived in Sterling, Massachusetts, US, around the early 18th century. She had a little lamb that accompanied her wherever she went, including to school! But the true history of the authorship of this popular rhyme is not mere child's play, involving legal battles in which even the automotive icon Henry Ford was involved at one stage! Moreover, this rhyme was the first recorded human voice on the first phonograph invented by Edison in 1877!

This article is dedicated to my grandchildren Maria and Serah. Maria will be celebrating her ninth birthday next month, while Serah turns 5 today. Yes, Mary had a little lamb in real life!

Maria & Serah

1806 - It starts with Mary Elizabeth Sawyer…

Mary Elizabeth Sawyer was born in 1806 on a farm in Sterling, Massachusetts. When she was 9 years old in 1815, while assisting her father on the farm, they discovered a sickly newborn lamb that had been abandoned by its mother. Mary persuaded her parents to allow her to hand-raise the lamb. Although they didn't expect the baby to survive for long, against all odds, Mary nursed the poor lamb back to health. Wherever Mary went, this lamb just followed, developing a special bond with her. As the lamb grew up, it had a fleece as white as snow!

The lamb used to follow Mary and her brother to the one-room school they attended, known as the Redstone School. Even in class, Mary had some embarrassing moments because of the lamb.

Redstone one-room school, which Mary and the lamb attended

One day, John Roulstone, a student of the same school but senior to Mary, wrote 3 stanzas of a poem based on the special relationship Mary and lamb had, as we all know.

Mary had a little lamb;

Its fleece was white as snow;

And everywhere that Mary went,

The lamb was sure to go.

It followed her to school one day

Which was against the rule;

It made the children laugh and play

To see a lamb at school

And so the teacher turned it out;

> But still it lingered near,
>
> And waited patiently about
>
> Till Mary did appear.

The lamb mothered 3 lambs of her own before she died. John Roulstone, too, suddenly died in 1822 at the age of 17 while he was at Harvard!

The Controversy Starts

In 1830, Sarah Josepha Hale, a renowned writer from Newport, published her book titled 'Poems for Our Children,' which included a version of the poem penned by John Roulstone! Sarah didn't make it clear how she could include a poem about Mary's lamb. Mary herself had no idea how Sarah had obtained Roulstone's poem! Mary lacked any proof other than her testimony. Although she had lost the handwritten poem, she had not lost the socks she had knitted from the wool of the very lamb that followed her to school. According to Mary Sawyer, the lamb was female, while Sarah Hale's poem depicts it as male!

Soon, the residents of Sterling, Massachusetts, and those from Newport, New Hampshire, were embroiled in arguments about the poem's origins for years. The dispute did not cease even after Sarah's death in 1879, followed by Mary's death in 1889!

The First Recording of a Human Voice

When Thomas Edison invented the phonograph in 1877, it was this poem that was recited for the first time! Yes, the first recording of human voice ever made was a recitation of the poem 'Mary Had a Little Lamb'!

 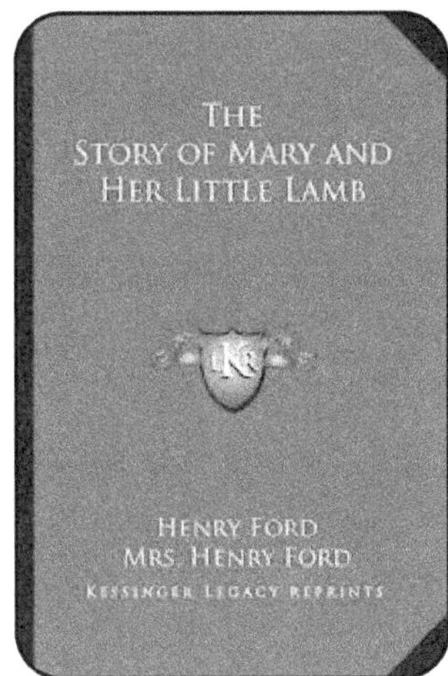

Mary Sawyer

Henry Ford Comes into the Picture

By 1920, Henry Ford openly supported Mary Sawyer. It was he who purchased the old school building where the lamb incident took place and relocated it to Sudbury, Massachusetts. The city authorities also ensured the preservation of Mary Sawyer's house to this day, where it stands now. Additionally, Ford published a book about Mary and the lamb!

Mary's house as seen today

It is Interesting to Note That a 2-foot-tall Statue of Mary's Lamb Stands in the Town Centre of Sterling!

Still an Outstanding Mystery

It is worth noting that nowhere could I find mention of the name of the lamb! After all, this lamb was a pet, and it is highly likely that Mary had given it a name. However, despite the story of the lamb later becoming controversial, I could not find its name mentioned in any records. Perhaps Maria, Serah, or any of my readers might discover it and inform me. Always remember that no topic is trivial. Interestingly, there is much to learn and understand in the world, even though many things may appear silly at first glance.

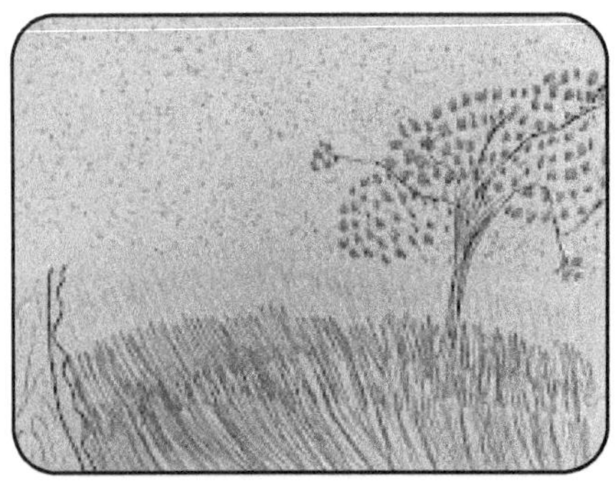

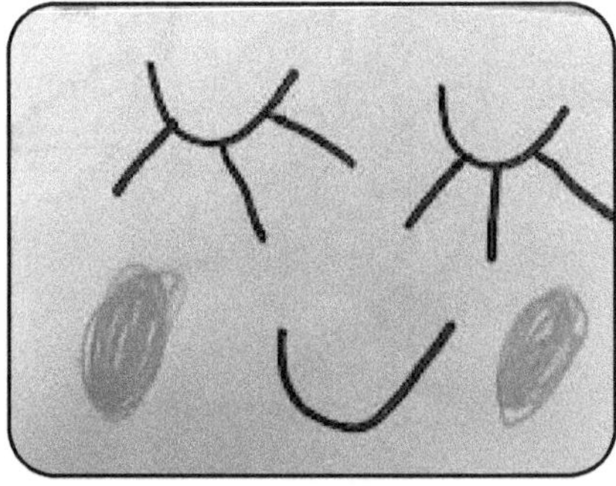

Be imaginative, creative, and inquisitive life is altogether different with these virtues.

AUSCHIWITZ! WHAT TO "B" REMEMBERED?

Auschwitz stands to this day as one of the most infamous camps of the Holocaust run by the Nazis- we all know that. More than 1.1 million Jews and a few others like gypsies, Polish and Soviet prisoners were murdered there in the cruellest ways for no fault of theirs. Nobody knows the actual figures but estimated a total of 1.5 million humans till January 1945, when the Soviet Army liberated the camp located in Poland.

But here I want to share with you something unknown about Auschwitz. When the SS, a dreaded Nazi outfit, ordered the poor prisoners to make a huge sign in metal, "ARBEIT MACHT FREI", above the main gate of the camp, meaning "work makes you free", - I don't think that anyone was set free working there hard! - the prisoners who worked on it turned the letter "B" upside-down without the notice of the Nazi bosses. As they were living in fear endlessly, humiliated and beatings before the murders of fellow prisoners they were forced to witness, this upside "B" was created to tell the world later what had actually happened at Auschwitz!

Yes. The upside-down "B", as predicted, now stands in many places of the world, exhibiting the undiluted exploitation of the weak and innocent! As the 78th anniversary of the liberation of this camp is approaching, it is also fair to remind ourselves how bad we can be given a chance.

The first 2 photos are from Auschwitz, while the third shows the one at Berlin!

Oswiecim Became Auschwitz

Auschwitz is located 40 km away from Krakow, Poland, which was annexed by Germany in 1939. It was a Polish military camp. The Nazis set up a refurbished camp for their prisoners since then, including gas chambers for extermination! The prisoners, mostly Jews, were brought to this camp by road and trains like packed sardines in a tin! The first thing after the prisoners reached the camp was to segregate them into old, young, sick, women and children. The old, women, sick, and children were immediately whisked away to gas chambers since otherwise they were to be fed! The rest were beaten, asked to work harder and harder, humiliated. The complex was huge, comprising 40 concentration and extermination camps. I don't want to write too much about the camp itself, which you might have read already. But I want to emphasise the fact that the Nazis did all these international operations of torture- including experimental ones of humans- without any publicity fearing a backlash from enemies.

But something haunts me after reflecting on what the poor prisoners, mostly Jews, went through. It is only 70-80 years since this horrific crime happened. Where were the political leaders of other nations then? What were the Christian spiritual leaders and leaders of other religions doing to stop this calamity perpetrated by Catholics? I am not writing about the merciless massacres of Genghis Khan in the 12th century either, but what happened in this modern world? I myself am a Christian, but I hang my head in shame with moist eyes and a guilty heart while contemplating what the poor souls endured.

Interestingly, this camp is now a major tourist attraction in Poland, exactly as the Nazis wanted! I shall elaborate more on the inverted "B."

The Auschwitz camp as it is seen today

"ARBEIT MACHT FREI"

It means "work sets you free" in German. In fact, it is a paraphrased quote from the Bible, specifically the Gospel of Saint John (18:32), which means "and you will know the truth and the truth will set you free." The Nazis manipulated this phrase to suit their intentions and convenience in many places, including all the concentration camps they established worldwide.

When the Polish workers were instructed by the SS to create the above sign in wrought iron over the gate, one worker named Jan Liwaez, a blacksmith, deliberately made the letter "B" upside-down to demonstrate his resistance without the notice of the SS! He sincerely believed that someone would later notice the mistake, and it would eventually reveal the hardships the prisoners had to endure, which the Nazis wanted to 'sweep under the carpet,' even after the war!

The 'Arbeit Macht Frei' sign was stolen in December 2010 but later recovered from the thieves, who were identified as neo-Nazi individuals from Sweden and Poland! Thereafter, it was returned to the Auschwitz museum, while a replica was placed on the gate!

WHAT TO REMEMBER?

Yes, we must remember that when injustices occur, when people are discriminated against and persecuted, we must never remain silent and indifferent. Indifference kills! Being an Indian whose ancestors endured centuries of slavery, oppression, and exploitation by colonial forces and others, this must be remembered at all costs.

"BE SURE TO PUT YOUR FEET IN THE RIGHT PLACE, THEN STAND FIRM!"

We cannot comprehend who people were once by looking solely at the zenith of their careers. A prime example is the current Prime Minister of India, Narendra Modi, who was once a tea seller but was recently witnessed by everyone delivering an unforgettable and impressive address to a Joint Session of the US Congress just a week ago! Regarding US presidents, there is no single career path to the White House and the American Presidency, although most of them were lawyers.

Americans seem to regard Abraham Lincoln not only as one of their great Presidents but also as a great man! I fully concur with them in this matter. The Emancipation Proclamation he issued on January 1, 1863, against all odds, stating that 'all persons held as slaves are, and henceforth shall be, free' is itself enough to make him great.

But how many of us know that Abraham Lincoln held various jobs before becoming President? He was a licensed bartender for a period, a part-owner of a small store in Illinois named Berry & Lincoln, and even a wrestling champion! Most interestingly, he was the only President to receive a patent, despite being a self-made person in education! Here, I am sharing 3 of his earlier jobs, which are less well-known: a bartender, a patent holder, and a wrestler.

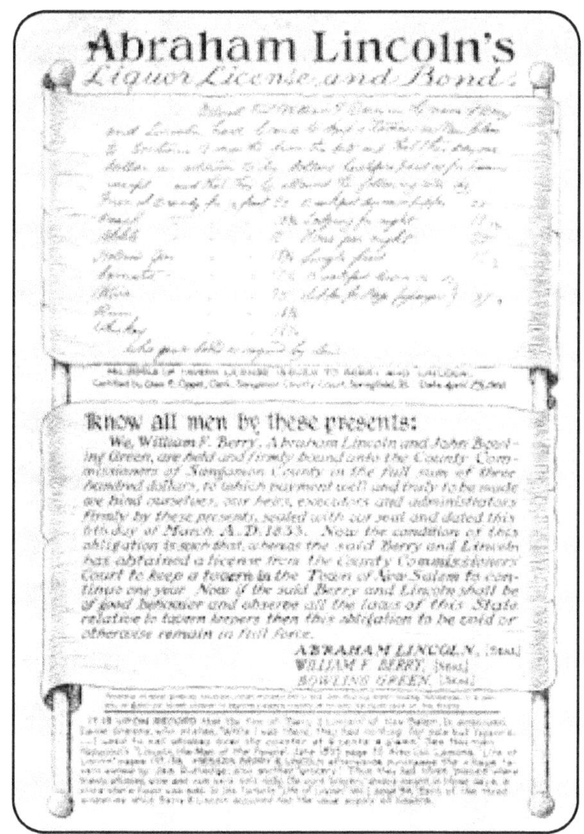

Abraham Lincoln's
Liquor License and Bond

Know all men by these presents:

We, William F. Berry, Abraham Lincoln and John Bowling Green, are held and firmly bound unto the County Commissioners of Sangamon County in the full sum of three hundred dollars, to which payment well and truly to be made we bind ourselves, our heirs, executors and administrators firmly by these presents, sealed with our seal and dated this 6th day of March A. D. 1833. Now the condition of this obligation is such that, whereas the said Berry and Lincoln has obtained a license from the County Commissioners Court to keep a tavern in the Town of New Salem to continue one year. Now if the said Berry and Lincoln shall be of good behavior and observe all the laws of this State relative to tavern keepers then this obligation to be void or otherwise remain in full force.

    ABRAHAM LINCOLN, (Seal)
    WILLIAM F. BERRY, (Seal)
    BOWLING GREEN, (Seal)

A Bartender

Abraham Lincoln served in the Black Hawk War, the conflict between the United States and Native Americans. It was after this that he met his friend, William F. Berry. Abraham Lincoln joined him in opening a store in Illinois at New Salem, where he lived from 1831 to 1837. Co-owned by his friend Berry, it was a general store licensed to sell alcohol in quantities greater than a pint for off-premises consumption.

Berry was an alcoholic and used to handle sales, while Lincoln dealt with customers and engaged in reading. As they fell into debt in 1833, Lincoln sold his interest to his partner and instead joined as a postmaster. Lincoln remained at New Salem, where he studied law and earned a legal licence.

A Patent Holder

Abraham Lincoln had a brief stint as a ferryman. His invention, "adjustable buoyant air chambers," could be attached to the sides of a boat. They could be lowered into the water and inflated to lift the boat over obstructions. On May 22, 1849, Lincoln was granted Patent No. 6469 for a device to lift boats over shoals, as described below.

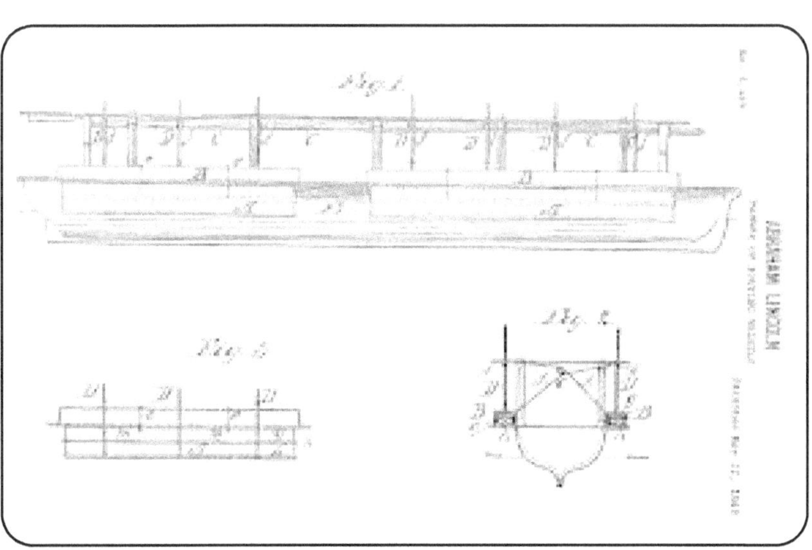

A Wrestler...

Wrestling was already an established sport among Native Americans in the 15th and 16th centuries when the first Europeans began arriving on the North American continent. Abraham Lincoln began wrestling as early as 1830, at the age of 21. Strengthened by physical hard work in the fields, Lincoln was an impressive physical specimen, standing at 6' 4" tall.

He completed over 300 wrestling matches over more than a decade and lost only once. He was the wrestling champion of his county in Illinois. While working in the store, he had a famous bout with Jack Armstrong, also a wrestling county champion. Few people know that Lincoln was enshrined in the National Wrestling Hall of Fame, along with a select few who became US presidents! See all the jobs Lincoln did before he became the great emancipator who said in his later life, "Be sure to put your feet in the right place, then stand firm!"

CLEOPATRA WAS NOT AN EGYPTIAN!

The box office hit movie 'Cleopatra' of 1963 still captivates me with its magnificent actors and scenes, even after 60 years. It was one of the costliest films ever produced, which led the producers into bankruptcy despite its success. The grand reception given to Queen Cleopatra and her son, Cesarian, from her union with Julius Caesar in Rome, is still worth viewing on YouTube even today! I am certain that anyone of my age who watched Elizabeth Taylor in the hit movie will always automatically remember her whenever they read about Cleopatra in later years! Perhaps I watched the movie one or 2 years later, in 1965 - I don't recall exactly - when it was released in my hometown, Kochi, which is blessed with world-class movie houses throughout India.

But here, I am not here to discuss the movie itself, but a fact I realised much later in life about Cleopatra. She was not Egyptian! Then what was she? She was of Macedonian Greek descent, for sure. She was indeed the Queen of Egypt, but not ethnically Egyptian! History clearly indicates that she was a member of the Ptolemaic dynasty, which ruled Egypt for 3 centuries after Alexander the Great, as she hailed from the family of those generals of Alexander. However, it is documented that she was the first ruler of her family to learn the Egyptian language, while her first language was Greek! Let my Egyptian friends forgive me if they are annoyed by this fact.

Cleopatra through the ages

Cleopatra may be a figure from ancient world history, but she still lives on in our minds as an iconic character. She is remembered for her beauty, her abilities as a queen, and her relationships with none other than Julius Caesar, who once ruled the world, and as the wife of Mark Antony! Writers have written about her, from Plutarch to William Shakespeare. She was the 'eternally enchanting beauty' for him. However, actual history indicates that most of these descriptions are exaggerated or even untrue! Firstly, she was never Egyptian! Her first language was Greek, although she spoke a dozen languages, including Egyptian. She was Queen of Egypt from 51 AD to 30 BC. Her first marriage was to her own brother, Ptolemy XIV. In 47 BCE, she gave birth to Ptolemy Caesar, supposedly fathered by Julius Caesar. She was the last ruler of Egypt before it was annexed by Rome.

Her Beauty

Historical accounts suggest that her intellectual abilities were more renowned during her time than her beauty. Her voice was recorded as extremely captivating in history. It is known that it was her voice that captivated Julius Caesar more than her beauty! Coins and other historical illustrations made during her time with her portraits clearly indicate this. Definitely, she was not anywhere close to resembling Elizabeth Taylor!

Coins showing Cleopatra, Julius Caesar and Mark Antony of their time

It is believed that it was the Arabs who conquered Egypt in 640 AD who began portraying her as a scholar, philosopher, and even a chemist.

Another part of history states that she ordered the murder of her own sister, Arsinoe so that she couldn't contest her rights as queen.

Cleopatra, Julius Caesar, and Mark Antony

Only a few know that Cleopatra was in Rome as the mistress of Julius Caesar when he was assassinated in 44 BC. She had to flee the city at that time.

Her relationship with Mark Antony seemed to be a perfect match. He sought access to the gold Egypt possessed, while she sought protection for herself and her family. Sadly, in 30 BC, Caesar Augustus, the emperor who came to power after Julius, also known as Octavian, declared them traitors and defeated them in a naval battle. Antony took a dagger to the stomach while Cleopatra took poison. Egypt was annexed to Rome thereafter.

Cecil B. DeMille and Cleopatra

Perhaps most of you are familiar with or have heard of Cecil B. DeMille. If not, you might have at least heard of one of his creations - The Ten Commandments, one of the best movies ever produced. He directed a film on Cleopatra as early as 1934, which was a hit.

DECODING EGYPTIAN HIEROGLYPHS!

For a layman, Egyptian Hieroglyphs look like an interesting piece of decorated art comprising hundreds of intricate and fancy symbols. These images include the sun, duck, eye, chairs, and feathers. but each has its own meaning and pronunciation! It is proven to be an ancient writing system leading to ancient Egypt from 3000 BC to 400 BC!

Egyptian hieroglyphs have Greek origin of the word - 'heiro' means sacred, while 'glyph' means 'to carve.' This pictorial language is believed to have been used for religious texts and funerary rituals that led to the legacies of Pharaohs! To know the importance of this ancient Egyptian wonder, we should note that it is pretty old, dating back to about 3000 years before Christ, and there was a decimal system of numeration up to a million!

Rosetta Stone

Rosetta is a town in Egypt, in the Nile Delta, about 65 km away from Alexandria. It is known as Rashid in Egypt. Probably without the discovery of the Rosetta stone, we would have remained ignorant about this ancient Egyptian language. During the Napoleonic war, a French captain discovered this stone at that place. This block of rock basalt he could identify with strange writings. Later, it was found to have 2 languages and 3 writing systems. The Rosetta stone is now housed in the British Museum.

Deciphering the stone was largely the work of 2 experts. One was Thomas Young of England, and the other was Jean Francois Champollion of France.

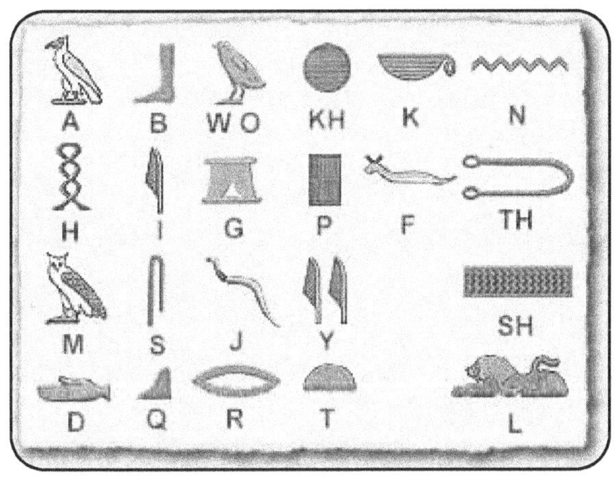

Jean Francois Champollion - The Father of Egyptology!

From childhood onwards, he was a child genius. By the age of 12, he had mastered 6 ancient Orient languages - Latin, Greek, Hebrew, Chaldean, Arabic, Coptic, and Syriac, other than the Egyptian language!

During the invasion of Napoleon in other countries, it was his practice to send an army of highly skilled professionals, including Mathematicians, Sculptors, Artists, Architects, Engineers, and others. Thus, Jean Francois also landed in Egypt. He conducted experiments and studies there on Egyptology. Once back in Paris, he was appointed as the first Curator of the collection of Egypt at The Louvre!

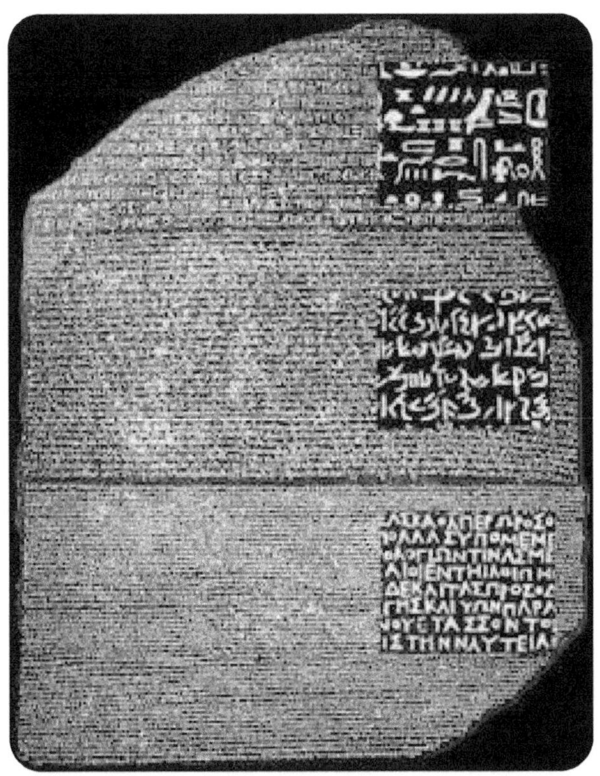

Rosetta Stone

On Sept 27, 1822, Jean Francois announced that he had decrypted the key of the Rosetta Stone, which led to detailed studies of ancient Egypt! AI - Artificial Intelligence is futuristic robots and computers that can think and act like humans. However, experts say that AI can be traced back to ancient Egypt and the use of hieroglyphs!

"DESPITE EVERYTHING, I BELIEVE THAT PEOPLE ARE REALLY GOOD AT HEART."

If you already know about Anne Frank, I'm not surprised. If not, you should. There could also be a section where people have heard of such a name but do not remember exactly how! "Sure, I have heard and read about her. But recently, I finally read her diary fully, which was so engaging for me. Even though she wrote this diary at age 13, living in constant fear, sadness, and horrors, her quotes show how resilience and optimism can sustain one through even the darkest times!

When Anti-Semitism took hold in Nazi Germany, Jewish Anne Frank, her sister Margot, and parents Otto and Edith left their home country for The Netherlands. Anne was just 5 years old then. She settled in the new place, learned the language, and made new friends. When the Nazis invaded The Netherlands in 1940, her parents decided to live in a secret annex where more such people took shelter. Anne started writing her diary then with quotes.

Eventually, after 2 years of hiding, she was caught along with her family members and sent to Auschwitz death camp. She had stopped writing her diary then, but it was found in safe custody. Her father Otto survived the horrors of the camp and published her diary in 1947 after the war. Anne was a nice girl next door but became famous all over the world once the diary hit the stands. Now she is an icon of peace and hope.

Anne Frank and the diary which was gifted to her.

From Frankfurt am Main to Amsterdam...

Anne Frank was born in 1929 in Frankfurt am Main, Germany. She had a sister Margot, who was 3 years older than her. As it was becoming difficult to live in Germany as Jews, Otto, her father, decided to migrate to The Netherlands along with family members to Amsterdam.

There too, Anne and her family couldn't live normally as the Nazis invaded The Netherlands on May 10, 1940. Otto tried to leave for England but failed. New laws were enforced in the country. Jews could not visit parks, cinemas, or even common shops since there were specific Jewish shops! They were forced to wear the Star of David as identification badges on all clothes. There were strong rumours that Jews would be taken out of the country and Anne Frank's family decided to go into hiding. Otto chose an old building for that which was named 'Secret Annex' by Anne in July 1942. In the old building, Otto ran an office and there was an old bookshelf which had secret access to a few rooms where the family lived at great risk. That's where she started writing in her diary which was presented on her 13th birthday.

Life At The "Secret Annex" Some of Her Quotes

For 2 years, the family lived there. It was during this period that Anne started recording her observations, feelings, quotes, and stories in the diary. I shall reproduce some of her famous quotes for your perusal:

"How wonderful it is that nobody need to wait a single moment before starting to improve the world."

"I don't think of all the misery but of the beauty that still remains."

"We aren't allowed to have any opinions. People can tell you to keep your mouth shut, but it doesn't stop you having your own opinion. Even if people are still very young, they shouldn't be prevented from saying what they think."

"What is done cannot be undone, but one can prevent it happening again."

"Writing in a diary is a really strange experience for someone like me. Not only because I've never written anything before, but also because it seems to me that later on neither I nor anyone else will be interested in the musings of a 13-year-old schoolgirl."

"Riches, prestige, everything can be lost. But the happiness in your own heart can only be dimmed; it will always be there, as long as you live, to make you happy again."

SS Arrests Anne Frank and Her Family

The whole family was arrested by Hitler's dreaded SS secret police on 4 August 1944. They were all taken to Auschwitz on a cattle train without any proper food or water. There, her father, Otto, was transferred to the male section while the other 3 were taken to a labour camp for women. Before long, Anne and her sister were transferred to another concentration camp, Bergen-Belsen, under terrible conditions. Anne and her sister contracted typhus and died in February 1945. Their mother was executed in the gas chambers of Auschwitz. Otto was miraculously rescued by the invading Russian Army.

Het Achterhuis Secret Annex

Anne Frank Becomes An Icon!

The diary left behind by Anne at the Secret Annex was rescued by Miep Gies, one of the Dutch citizens who hid Anne Frank and her family. Once the war was over, she passed the diary to Otto. Upon reading it, Otto realised that it was no ordinary diary or quotes from a thirteen-year-old girl. With requests, compulsion, and help from his friends, he published it as a book titled "Het Achterhuis" in Dutch in June 1947 with around just 3000 copies. It was an instant hit. Thereafter, it was translated into more than 70 languages and also adapted for screen and stage. The Secret Annex, the hiding place, became a museum in 1960! There are a number of movies available on OTT platforms based on the story of Anne Frank.

Arguably, Anne Frank became the most well-known of the 6 million Jews who died in the Holocaust!

DID COLUMBUS DISCOVER AMERICA? THEN HOW DID THE COUNTRY GET THE NAME AMERICA?

When Americans get a holiday on every 10th October since 1937 to celebrate as 'Columbus Day', why should I doubt? Americans and Europeans can never go wrong in anything, especially the narration of their own history, don't you think so? Nevertheless, the fact that Christopher Columbus never set foot on or discovered North America in any of his voyages is a historical fact. Then who else? Amerigo Vespucci, whose name gave the country and 2 continents their names - America? He did not land in North America at any time either! Was it Leif Ericson, the Icelandic Viking explorer who is believed to have reached Newfoundland, Canada some 500 years before Columbus? No, as he too failed to reach the American mainland.

Interestingly, as we all know, Columbus was keen to find a new sea route to reach India for trading its riches along with the Indies and China. Finally, when Columbus reached the islands like the Bahamas and Hispaniola (Haiti and the Dominican Republic as known today), he sincerely believed that he had reached India and that the people there were called Indians! This fact is too well-known to be repeated here.

When Amerigo Vespucci reached South America and the Amazon River, he named that spot of the Amazon as the 'Gulf of Ganges' since he too believed that he had reached India

and the Ganges! I am sure that this is not well-known in history.

This is not history reinvented but revisited. It was there all along but many of us must not have noticed or wrongly observed for obvious reasons!

Columbus Makes 4 Trips But None Touched The Mainland Of The USA!

During the 15th and 16th centuries, Europeans, especially Spanish, Portuguese, Dutch, and others, wanted to find sea routes to India, China, and the Far East. Their main intention was to bring back cargoes of spices and silks to become quickly rich.

Christopher Columbus was born in Genoa, Italy, but later moved to Lisbon, Portugal. Columbus knew that the earth was round unlike the Catholic theologians of those days who insisted that the earth was flat! He calculated that sailing West instead of East around Africa would eventually lead to India. Finally, the King and Queen of Spain, Ferdinand and Isabella, agreed to finance Columbus's trip.

Columbus travelled in 1492 in the ship named 'Santa Maria' along with 2 other ships - the Nina and the Pinta - similar ships and a crew of 90 from Palos, Spain for sure.

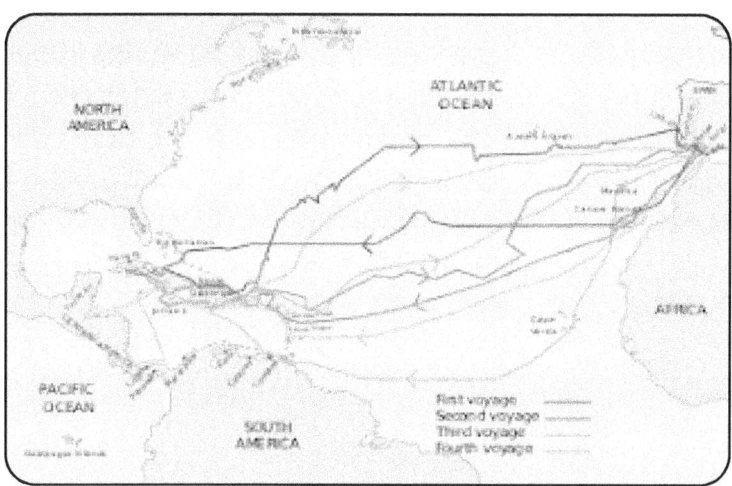

Between 1492 and 1504, Columbus made 4 trips of expeditions of discovery to India and the Indies, which was later known as the Age of Discovery. Although he didn't touch the mainland of America as seen in the map above, these voyages led to widespread knowledge of the new world! The Bahamas as well as the Caribbean islands are known to this day as the West Indies. It is also to be noted here that Columbus was merciless, brutally enslaving the natives (thinking that they were Indians) in these expeditions! He died in 1506 with the belief that he had discovered a new sea route to India!

Amerigo Vespucci Made 2 Trips but Again Did not Touch America!

Vespucci played a major role in at least 2 voyages in search of India between 1499 and 1502, reaching present-day South America. He was from Italy and by profession a cartographer. In 1499 when he sailed to the Amazon River, he named it the 'Gulf of Ganges' thinking that he had reached India! In history, it is recorded that Vespucci had met Columbus at least once in 1496 and shared experiences, but both never landed in the United States Of America!

In 1507, Martin Waldseemüller, a German clergyman and another famous cartographer, first used the name America in honour of Amerigo Vespucci, and it became associated with the 2 new continents and the country. He was the first to make a new map of the world separating America from Asia. In the US, every March 9 is observed as Amerigo Vespucci day officially but with much less fanfare and celebration compared to Columbus Day, I believe.

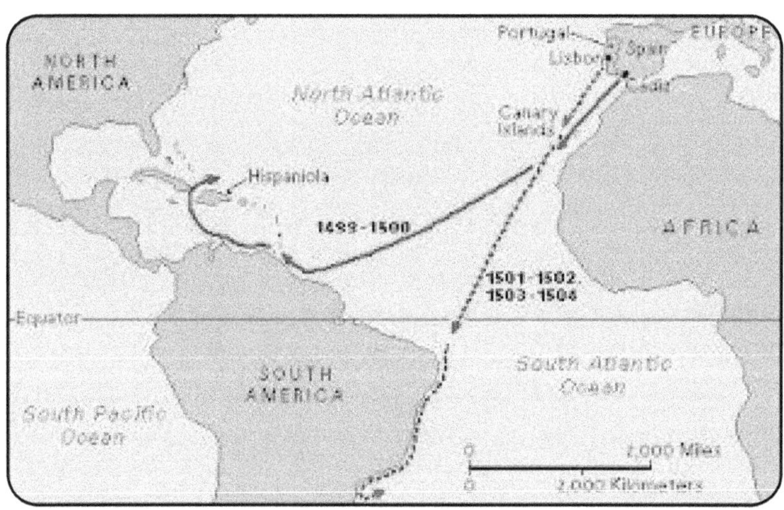

The Voyage Of Leif Erikson

About 500 years earlier than the expeditions of Columbus and Vespucci, an Icelandic Viking explorer had surely made a voyage from his home country in search of the new world. It is recorded in history that he had established a settlement at Vinland in Newfoundland, Canada. It was US President Coolidge who recognised the feat of Leif Erikson in 1925 and declared October 9 as Leif Erikson Day.

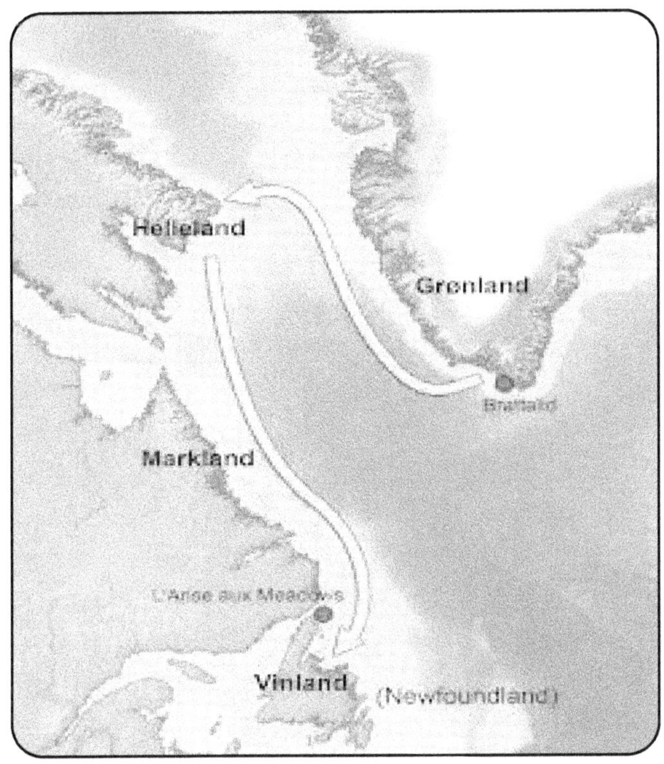

Helleland
Grønland
Brattalid
Markland
L'Anse aux Meadows
Vinland
(Newfoundland)

DOLMEN OF MARAYOOR!

Since we came back from Doha and resettled in our hometown of Kochi, Geetha and I have been visiting many states of India that we have not seen so far. So also places within our own state. Travel has always been one of our passions. Soon, we could regroup with 3 more old friends - the late Govindan Kutty, Cherian and Venugopal, classmates of mine at the Engineering College hailing from the same city who have similar tastes and interests. Moreover, we all were working initially in India but spent the heyday of our careers in the Arabian Gulf states, which was another catalyst to make our relationships warm. Along with them and their better halves, we could make a lot of trips within our own state, the rest of India and abroad. One such trip was specific for Marayoor, the only place in Kerala known for natural sandalwood forests. It is also known for 'Neelakurinji' flowers, which blossom only once in 12 years! But we could end up visiting something I hardly knew of -Dolmen of pre-historic days.

Situated at +5000 ft above MSL, Marayoor can be reached by serpentine roads about 50 km away from Munnar, the famous hill station. Due to its location and climatic conditions, Marayoor is the only place in Kerala where Apples, Oranges, strawberries, Blackberries, Plums and Peaches are grown. Dolmens of Marayoor are locally known as 'Muniyara', meaning dens of sages. The way these Dolmens are kept, or, I would say, neglected by the Govt and public, I am sure that people over here are not fully aware of our own values in history. These

Dolmen could be the earliest monuments of its kind existing in the state or one of such in India and the rest of the world!

Dolmen In India

About these Dolmens, I had read about them years ago somewhere, but not much. As we walked up the steep hill, enjoying the cool afternoon breeze, and reached the site, I could see quite a number of such Dolmens. Dolmens are burial chambers of the prehistoric age meant for Individuals of higher status in society. They were buried in a sitting position. Even now, this practice continues among certain communities in India. The larger the chamber, the more important the person would have been. They are constructed of 4 stones placed on edges with a larger stone used as 'a capstone', which are called megaliths. With the Anamudi hill in the distant background, the sight of hundreds of such stone chambers all around is a scene that we will remember for a long time to come.

These Dolmens belong to the Neolithic age—a term used to describe the period when humans transitioned from hunting wild animals to cultivating plants for sustenance—dating from 4000 BC to 2000 BC. It appears that many anthropologists and archaeologists from around the world visit this location. However, the site is completely neglected by the authorities!

While Kerala remains the state with the highest number of Dolmens in India, they are also found in Tamil Nadu, Andhra Pradesh, Karnataka, and Maharashtra.

Dolmens Abroad

Dolmen are known to exist in Japan, Russia, South Korea, Ireland, Israel, Jordan and China. In North Africa and European countries, too, they exist. The maximum number (35000) is found in South Korea, which UNESCO has declared a heritage site.

In olden times, people were superstitious and believed that those Dolmens were creations of giants or even devils! A few centuries back, some anthropologists shared the view that these Dolmens were creations of certain Aegean tribes, which was proved to be wrong later. Now that it is proven to be scientifically by the 14 C radiocarbon method, which has been available since 1940, the oldest is believed to be in central Europe/Northern Europe. I am not ready to buy this 'historical story' readily since the Europeans will go to any extent to showcase that they have a superior past compared to others! Moreover, I simply believe that the past history of India and elsewhere in Asia was much superior to those of Europeans, although the latter happened to colonise and steal all the resources of Asians!

One of the Dolmen preserved in South Korea

The absence of any metal indicates the age of the Dolmen. The famous Stonehenge in the UK is not a Dolmen in the strictest sense, but it is certainly constructed using stones, including Dolmens! Other older megalithic sites in the world include Gobekli Tepe (Turkey), Alit Yama (Israel), the Carnac stones (France), and the Pyramids, you know where they are!

EVER ROLLING BUST OF WINSTON CHURCHILL AND 'BEASTLY' INDIA!

One interesting incident happened -still it goes in the Oval Office- that made me write about Winston Churchill. He is considered a great prime minister, war hero, and leader who has contributed immensely to his country, the United Kingdom. In India, too, his proficiency in English literature is appreciated by many. For me, he is considered to be an undiluted racist.

In 2001, Tony Blair, PM of the UK, presented a sculptured bust of Winston Churchill during a visit to the Oval Office of the President of the United States while George w Bush was in the chair. Bush adorned his office, giving it a prominent place. In 2009, when President Obama came to power, he ordered the removal of this bust from his office and moved it elsewhere in the White House. Surely, he didn't want to see the face of Churchill every day! His strange act could have triggered a low-level US-UK relationship, though apparently, the UK said it is the US President's freedom! But the episode did not stop there. In 2017, when Donald Trump came to the seat, he asked his personnel staff to replace the bust to the Oval Office, only to be again taken out by President Joe Biden in 2021! I am sure that this is not the end of the story but only the beginning of the story, which may be reflected in the coming decades as well!

Why America, or at least a good section of them, don't respect Churchill, which Indians apparently don't? He was an incorrigible racist, and he got such a negative remark

based on his attitude towards India and Indians. "I hate Indians. They are a beastly people with a beastly religion. The famine (1943) was their fault for breeding like rabbits" This was one side of Churchill about whom we should all know, not to avenge or reciprocate but to learn from what has been going on!

My Close Associations With The British

During my time in Qatar, I had the opportunity to interact with numerous British individuals, hailing from various regions of the UK—England, Wales, Scotland. Among them were highly educated professionals, as well as individuals with minimal education masquerading as professional managers in state-run oil corporations and government services, especially during the nineteen-eighties. Additionally, I had the privilege of knowing British diplomats and commercial attaches, acquaintances made through the contacts of the chairman of the commercial group I was associated with. He was a career diplomat and ambassador of Qatar and Scandinavian countries for an extended period. Furthermore, I frequently met and interacted with regular visitors from the UK who came to Qatar as consultants, general managers, or marketing managers. Overall, my impressions of them were generally good.

But I later came to understand that there is still a significant percentage of them who are racists in the UK, still influenced by the legacy of their past domination of the seven seas and the colonisation of many countries across all continents. India was a prized possession, as they systematically siphoned off the rich resources of that colonial nation to their royal coffers, estimated to be a staggering $45 billion! The GDP per capita of Britain soared from a mere $1400 in 1750 (when the East India Company entered India) to $7000 in 1947 (when the British were compelled to leave India)! This represents a fivefold increase over 197 years, achieved through nothing more than the exploitation of India! You can see for yourself how the curve below takes off from 1850 for the UK, while it remains a straight line for poor India. I always believed that the Indians of those days were naively foolish to allow British traders to dominate them. Moreover, many British politicians and officials of that era viewed Indians as unintelligent and racially inferior, without considering the consequences or what lay in store for them. Winston Churchill was such an individual—a racist as abhorrent as Hitler!

Please refer to the second graph, illustrating how 'beastly' India overtakes the UK in GDP! I can assure you that this is only the start for India.

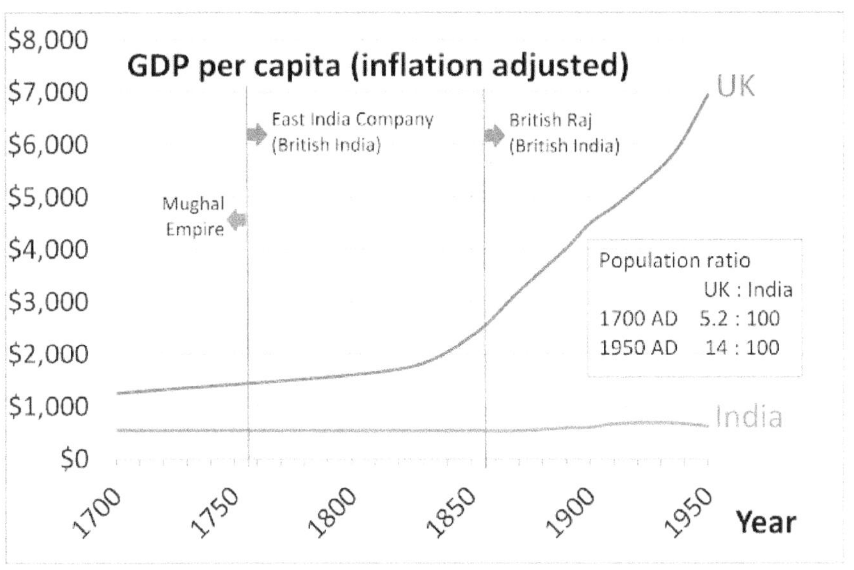

How the GDP of UK went up while they were ruling India

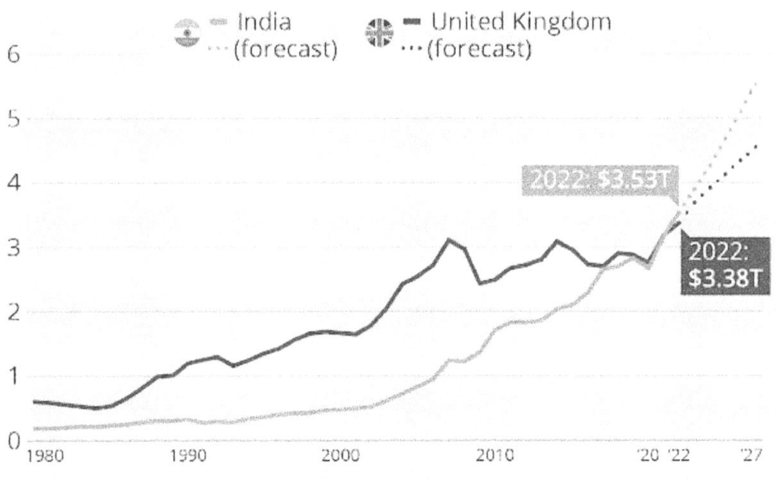

In spite of the loot from India, see how 'beastly' India overtakes UK in GDP

Quotes of Winston Churchill

I shall simply quote what Churchill said or wrote without any bias:

1. "It is alarming and nauseating to see Mr. Gandhi, a seditious Middle Temple lawyer, now posing as a fakir, striding half-naked up the steps of the Viceregal palace!" This is what he said about Mahatma Gandhi in 1931.

2. In 1937, his remarks about Americans and Australians may not be as well-known. "I do not admit, for instance, that a great wrong has been done to the Red Indians of America or the black people of Australia. I do not admit that a wrong has been done to these people by the fact that a stronger race, a higher-grade race, a more worldly-wise race, to put it, has come in and taken their place." Hitler also shared similar sentiments, as do many white Americans and Australians even today!

3. In 1954, regarding Chinese Communists, he wrote, "I hate people with slit eyes and pigtails."

His comments about Islam were also derogatory. Although he did not oppose Judaism, he harboured reservations about Jews 'only helping each other'! According to him, 'White Protestant Christians are at the top, above white Catholics, while Indians are higher than Africans'. He viewed himself and Britain as winners in a social Darwinian hierarchy!

Nobel Prize in English Literature And The Bengal Famine

In 1953, Winston Churchill was awarded the Nobel Prize in English Literature. Interestingly, it was conferred "for his mastery of historical and biographical description, as well as for brilliant oratory in **defending exalted human values**," as stated by the Nobel Foundation. Meanwhile, Mahatma Gandhi was conveniently overlooked for the Nobel Prize for Peace during his lifetime.!

For me, he was a BIG FROG in a SMALL POND, mistakenly believing it to be an ocean! He was a staunch Imperialist who firmly believed in the superiority of the British Empire. Due to his misguided policies in Bengal, 3 million impoverished Indians perished from hunger and disease during the famine of 1943.

courtesy: the graphs for google.

EVOLUTION OF TIRANGA - THE INDIAN NATIONAL FLAG - OVER THE YEARS

My interest in the growth, development and affairs of my own mother country might have grown many folds during and after my stay as an expatriate in a foreign country. Getting a chance to meet and closely interact with so many different nationals in a Gulf state that was undergoing a fast-developing economy was a sort of eye-opener and catalyst for learning about others firsthand. It also gave me a chance to compare my own professional skills with other nationals. That was a period before when a US President declared to his fellow men that his country was having inflation since Indians started 'eating' food! Or another President was scared of losing IT jobs in the US since they were getting outsourced to Bangalore or, simply as he put it, 'Bangalored'! It also gave me a chance to introspect - to compare what is India and Indians with others. Before I could return for good only, I came to a conclusive finding that in spite of many shortcomings, India is great comparatively. And the worst impacts of colonisation are over, and brighter days are ahead for India.

Once I returned for a retired, relaxed life in Kochi, my home town, one of the opportunities I never gave up on was hoisting a Tiranga-Indian tricolour flag on every Independence day at my own residence. I used to do that myself the night before itself and put off the porch light so that it is visible in the early morning to all those who pass by! I don't know why, but that's an act I enjoy silently to this day. I might have got a shot in my arm, an injection of ' patriotism' from my expatriate days!

Recently, I accidentally happened to learn about the evolution of the flag of a western country but thought that I should learn about our own Tiranga (Tri coloured) first, then others, which I did. Definitely, I know all Indians have a knowledge of the same, but I assure you that there are many more historical facts, that actually happened, much more than what you and I know.

The role of British, American and Irish Nationals Who Were Genuine Lovers Of India

We often think only about the looting by the British in India, but we forget that there were at least a few British individuals who contributed to India's freedom struggle and the welfare of Indians. Annie Besant, B.G. Horniman, Philip Spratt, Madelina Slade (Mira), R.R. Keithahn, C.F. Andrews, Catherine Mary Heileman (Sarla). There was also another American who languished in an Indian jail for our freedom - Samuel Stokes. I am sure that generations born after 1947, like myself, may not even be aware of these names. I wanted to add A.O. Hume, the British civil servant who founded the Congress Party, to the list. However, since he is accused of playing the role of a 'double agent' - described as a 'safety valve' to give Indians an outlet for resentment after the 1857 Indian Mutiny - including freedom fighters like Lala Lajpat Rai and Dadabhai Naoroji, I refrain from doing so. Then there is the role of Margaret Elizabeth Noble, more popularly known as Sister Nivedita, an Irish woman.

Sr. Nivedita flag (1904)

As India was always a single country, albeit with different dynasties and kingdoms, each with its own flag, before independence, Indians never felt the need for a unified flag during that time.

The first attempt to design a national flag came from Sister Nivedita, originally Irish, who was a disciple of Swami Vivekananda as early as 1904. Two colours - red and yellow- were used, representing the freedom struggle and victory, respectively. The words "Vande Mataram," meaning "bow to thee" in Bengali, were boldly written on it with a figure of the vajra, the weapon of the God Indra. It was a square flag.

National Day of Mourning and Parsi Bagh Square flag (1906)

On 16th October 1905, the British government unilaterally decided to partition Bengal. Probably this unexpected move was the first impetus for Indian nationalists to have a national thinking and a national flag for themselves. The day of partition was proclaimed to be a 'National' Day of Mourning. In 1906, Sachindra Prasad Bose and Hemchandra Kaungo, 2 socialists from Bengal, designed the first tricoloured flag, which was unfurled on 7th August 1906 at Parsi Bagh Square, Calcutta.

The flag had 8 lotuses representing the number of provinces the British ruled then, a crescent, and a sun. "Vande Mataram" was written at the centre.

Bhikaji Cama's Flag (1907) Bhikaji

Cama was an Indian Parsi lady in exile living in Paris. She, along with Shyamji Krishna Verma and Vinayak Damodara Savarkar, redesigned the same flag that was earlier unfurled in Calcutta in 1906 with some changes as below.

The red colour was replaced with saffron. 8 lotuses were changed to 1 lotus and 7 stars denoting Saptarshi or 7 sages mentioned in the Vedas. Madame Cama unfurled the same flag in Germany at Stuttgart in a Socialist gathering, the first time such an Indian flag was seen in a foreign country.

Home Rule flag (1917)

Dr. Annie Besant and Lokmanya Tilak designed a new flag during the Home Rule movement. I believe the American flag might have influenced them.

Five red and 4 horizontal strips and seven stars of Saptarshi with a crescent and Union Jack were the main features.

The flag of 1921 by Pingali Venkaiah The final version of India's national flag can be traced to the design of Pingali Venkaiah of Andhra Pradesh. His proposal, which had only 2 colours- red and green- was presented to Mahatma Gandhi during a Congress Working Committee meeting, representing 2 major communities of India, Hindus and Muslims. On Gandhi's recommendation, a third colour was added - white, representing other minorities. Also, a spinning wheel was placed at the centre.

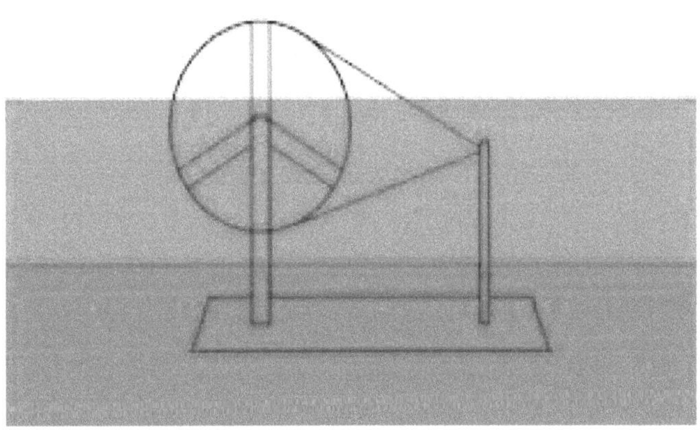

The Year 1931 Flag Committee's Swaraj Flag

The flag committee of Congress finally approved a tricoloured flag with a few major changes, as shown below. The red was replaced by saffron, the position of white was changed to the middle, and a charkha or spinning wheel was placed on the white band without mentioning any representation of specific communities.

1947 Flag on Independence Day

Finally, the Constituent Assembly adopted the tricolour flag of 1931 with a major change of the Dharma Chakra of Emperor Ashoka in the centre replacing the spinning wheel.

The First Flag Hoisted in India

The first flag of India on Indian soil was hoisted on December 30, 1943, by Netaji Subhash Chandra Bose at Port Blair, Andamans, which could be a little-known twist in the history of India. Interestingly, he also unfurled the tricolour flag with a tiger in the centre at a place still known as Flag Point on the island.

Pingali Venkaiah

Now, how many Indians remember this man who was the basic architect of India's tricolour flag, who died a poor man in 1963? In 2009, I understood that his name was proposed by his state of birth, Andhra Pradesh, to honour him as Bharat Ratna, but the central government chose to honour him by issuing a stamp.

FEW SCOOPFULS OF MUSINGS

Stories of successful businesses worldwide have always interested me. There is always something to learn, even from failed businesses, especially from fellow competitors.

The most important aspect of establishing and running a successful business of any end product or service is to know more about the customer and then learn how to sell to them. It may seem simple, but it is very difficult to put into practice, as I could understand firsthand in my career. Even an established business has to continue satisfying the interests of the customer to remain in business.

Here, I am presenting a successful business story of an ice cream brand, an FMCG product. Though now a well-known international brand, it had very humble origins in the US, where it consumes the maximum ice creams in the world. Produced from a small setup in 1976 in the Bronx, NY, it unusually used a Danish-sounding name for a peculiar reason, which essentially clicked. Here is the story of Häagen-Dazs. As one of their advertisement captions from years back, I have based it as a title!

The Origin

Hardly anyone knows that the origin of ice cream in the world is not Italy or anywhere in Europe. Right from King Solomon to Alexander the Great, many used to enjoy ice cream, though not in the form which we use now. Surprisingly, it is China from where it is believed that the great traveller Marco Polo brought the recipe to Italy! Ice cream is very common among all the people in the world, but New Zealand, the US, and Australia top the list of consumers - in that order.

The First Ice Cream Café in the World

It was in Paris that the first such café was opened in 1651! Café Procope, named after its Sicilian Chef, is recorded. It was a hit, with more than 250 such outlets springing up in the city within the next 50 years! However, it had to be closed in 1872 and reopened only in 1920!

Le Procope, Paris as seen today

The café was frequented by La Fontaine, Voltaire, Benjamin Franklin, Danton, Marat, Robespierre, Napoleon Bonaparte, Balzac, Victor Hugo, Gambetta, Verlaine, as written on a plaque exhibited to this day.

In the US

It was Quaker colonists who introduced ice cream to the US in 1744. It is recorded that Benjamin Franklin, George Washington, and Thomas Jefferson were known ice cream lovers among the Presidents of the USA. The first ice cream shop was established in New York in 1777, but it was in 1851 that a milk dealer named Jacob Russell began manufacturing ice cream as an industry. He did this in Baltimore.

The Name Häagen-Dazs Emerges

Reuben and Rose Mattus were a Polish couple who immigrated to the US. In 1961, they introduced a new luxury ice cream. The reason for a Danish-sounding name was to honour the country that did so much for the Jewish People during the Holocaust rather than for any commercial reasons. I remember 'Anne Frank and her diary' in this context. Otherwise, it is an all-out American brand. The very name was chosen by the owners to suggest foreign and exotic origins! Reuben was sure that such a catchy foreign name would attract Americans based on his marketing experience with frozen refreshments.

Quality is Always the Winner

The owners of Häagen-Dazs always believed that there would be customers who would seek quality products. Therefore, they never engaged in price wars with competitors, as there would be customers willing to pay a little extra for quality. This is something I always practised as a CEO successfully. At times, I had differences of opinion on this matter with the chairman of the company, but it did not dent my faith in the extra quality of products for a little extra money. Ultimately, we gained clientele who appreciated quality and professionalism, which became the official motto of the company!

The first exclusive Haagen Dazs parlour is still in use in Bronx, NY.

From inception onwards, Häagen-Dazs went for genuine products of quality with 'no preservatives, no artificial colours, no stabilisers, and no additives!'

By 1980, Häagen-Dazs had become one of the elite brands of ice creams. With Reuben and Rose both in their seventies, they thought it was time to sell the company in 1983. Pillsbury agreed to buy it for $75 million! Selecting a name without a meaning in 1961, they created meaning over the years - it means the best!

"FOR THE LOVE OF COFFEE," FROM PADRE FRANCISCO ROMERO TO JUAN VALDEZ

Which country has the best coffee in the world? I am not an expert in the field, but I would argue that it is Colombia based on authentic statistics and unbiased information available on the subject. The Colombian landscape provides the perfect natural environment for growing coffee, along with its climate, among 80 countries which grow coffee. The quality of coffee is also influenced by a variety of factors such as soil, altitudes above sea level, etc., making Colombia responsible for filling up 15% of the world's consumption with its own Arabica.

But what interests me are 2 factors - one historical and the other commercial - which influenced Colombia in its production of coffee beans. The first is about Francesco Romero, a Jesuit priest visiting Colombia in the 18th century. Convinced about what wonders coffee could do for the people and the country, he used the most unconventional religious method to spread coffee plantations among people who were reluctant to plant coffee beans!

Second is how Colombia professionally marketed its coffee to reach the world by inventing and promoting a fictional Colombian coffee farmer named Juan Valdez with his mule in 1959. Both are incredible but true.

Coffee Revolution in Colombia

It started with a Jesuit priest named Francisco Romero from Spain visiting the country in the 18th century. Coffee had reached Colombia before that, but the farmers were reluctant to plant them considering the fact that it takes not less than 5 years for the coffee plants to bear fruits for the first crop - a pretty long time for the poor farmers.

Convinced about the development coffee plantations could bring to families and society under the best climatic environments ideally suited for coffee to grow, it is believed that this priest devised a trick with the believers. Instead of the usual penance at confession in the church, he told them to plant coffee plants. He promised them in the name of God that their sins would be absolved in exchange. The penance could vary between 100 or 1000 bushes depending on the seriousness of the sin committed.

This reminds me of the 'sale of indulgences' by Pope Leo X in 1517 to raise funds to build St. Peter's Basilica in Rome! While this act resulted in the movement of Reformation by Martin Luther and ultimately led to the split of the church, the act of Francisco Romero made a positive revolution for Colombia. As a priest, he was present in all the places of Colombia, but he started promoting the cultivation of coffee at Salazar de las Palmas. Within a few years after the death of Francisco Romero in 1865, Colombia started exporting coffee!

What Juan Valdez and his mule Conchita Did

The National Federation of Coffee Growers of Colombia, as early as 1959, took steps to bring Colombian coffee to the international market. They entrusted the famous US ad firm named Doyle Dane Bernbach (DDB) for this purpose. Thus, the fictional coffee farmer Juan Valdez was born in Manhattan, NY, created by William Bernbach, the founder of DDB. Juan Valdez was also given a companion, a mule named Conchita. Valdez and Conchita captured the hearts of American coffee lovers. Just 5 months after the first Juan Valdez commercial was introduced in the US, the sale of Colombian coffee there increased by a whopping 300%, to the astonishment of even DDB. Within a few years, it became a household name in America!

Initially, the role of Juan Valdez - dressed in the classic outfit of the Colombian coffee region - was played by a Cuban named Jose Duval. He was succeeded by Carlos Sanchez from Colombia until 2006. Now it is portrayed by Carlos Castaneda, an actual coffee grower from Colombia! Juan Valdez is always seen with his pet donkey Conchita carrying 2 bags full of coffee beans on its sides. Such animals are favourites in the hilly coffee regions of Colombia as companions of farmers.

There are over 335 Juan Valdez coffee shops in Colombia and around 150 abroad. There is one at Katara Cultural Centre in Doha, Qatar, but none in India yet, I presume. They may be under the impression that all Indians are 'chai' lovers, but South India, especially Chennai, could challenge this belief!

No wonder coffee became the second most consumed beverage in the world after water!

FORGET THE LOTTERY. BET ON YOURSELF.

For the last few decades, passing through international airports without being tempted to buy a lottery ticket has been difficult for me. There are quite a few duty-free shops in airports which offer a one-in-5000 chance to win a prize money of $1 million (Rs. 8.20 Cr) with no restrictions on the number of tickets one can purchase! Even while at bus stations and railway stations in India, once every 5 minutes, a seller approaches you with a lottery ticket. Winning a lottery is anyone's dream! Almost.

I never had any such temptation from day one. As such, I have hardly purchased such lottery tickets in my life simply because it is a sort of gambling like Poker, Horse racse, or slot machines in which I don't indulge either. Thankfully, I remember now how my parents and even grandparents have taught me to remain so. This has nothing to do with the money and possessions one has because I have seen people who are filthy rich or utterly poor going mad after lottery tickets and other gambling ways! When I married, the fact that I got a partner who has been brought up in the same way as I am in this matter made my life easier.

I used to think that the lottery was a capitalist idea in the modern world, but in Communist China, too, it is rampant. Greed for easy money is simply human, and exploitation of the weak-minded is another human trait! Here I am trying to make a fast trail of the lottery in the world, in spite I believe in the famous words of Brian Koslow, which is reflected in the title. Then why is a picture of the Great Wall of China given here?

The Largest Gambling Population

Before I dig out the history, let me note down the first 5 countries in the world with the largest gambling population now. They are Singapore, with three-fourths of the population regularly gambling, Finland, with one-third of the population, Australia, Ireland, and the UK. Ironically, Singaporeans are considered to be among the best among humans now for IQ! In Singapore, Singapore Pools, a government-owned lottery subsidiary, is licensed to run the lotteries. However, the biggest lottery jackpots are from the US and Europe.

How It Started in the World

The credit for operating the first lottery is recorded in history about 200 years before the Birth of Christ. The Hans dynasty of China introduced the first lottery in the world with the aim of raising funds for building the Great Wall of China. In ancient Rome, Emperor Augustus also introduced a lottery system to maintain roads. During the 1700s, many of the elite learning institutions of the American Ivy League raised funds for new buildings through lotteries, including Yale and Harvard!

The oldest lottery still active today is the Dutch National lottery. Since 1726, this has been ongoing in The Hague. The next one is 'El Gordo' (meaning the fat one) in Spain since 1812, which is also considered to be one of the biggest lotteries in the world. The Powerball Lottery of the US holds the world's record for the largest prize ever awarded - $2.04 billion!

Las Vegas is a City That Never Sleeps!

A lottery is a form of gambling for sure, although many Governments patronise them. Basically, they encourage people to pay a small sum of money with a chance to win a big jackpot. I have seen myself as the poorest expatriate worker and the rich class, including filthy rich Arabs queuing up for such lottery tickets at the airports! This human weakness is well taken into account in Las Vegas, the biggest and largest gambling centre in the world.

Although my wife and I are not interested in gambling of any sort, we visited the place, also known as the 'City of Sins' and stayed there, which is now equally known for shopping, entertainment, fine dining, and nightlife. The buffet breakfasts, lunches, and dinners the hotels offer there could be the ultimate in that respect, I remember. One will get lost in the midst of the variety of foods displayed but at the same time organised very orderly. A night ride in a helicopter viewing that city which never sleeps is something unforgettable.

FROM NAZI TO NASA, US AND ROSCOSMOS, RUSSIA

HOW V2 - THE NAZI ROCKET AND SCIENTISTS WERE USED BY AMERICANS AND RUSSIANS IN SPACE WAR.

October 4, 1957. Moscow time is 10.29 PM. As Russia launched the first artificial satellite named 'Sputnik 1' - meaning fellow traveller in the Russian language - the US, the West, and the rest of the world were taken aback by surprise! The Russian (Soviet) news agency TASS and Radio Moscow announced that the successful launch could be seen with the use of powerful binoculars and even record the Beep-Beep signal using appropriate instruments! As the scientists and others in the US watched and listened in awe, mixed with panic rather than happiness, this Soviet spacecraft passed over them many times a day. The space war between Russia and the US had begun that day during another already ongoing war - the Cold War.

Before the excitement over Sputnik 1 was over, the Russians fired the 'Sputnik 2' just after 4 weeks, on November 3, 1957! The world got bewildered, knowing that a dog named 'Laika' too was sent in it into orbit, making it the first living creature ever to do so. On May 15, 1958, 'Sputnik 3' was launched with a lot of instruments fitted on them, though other than the Russians, nobody knew precisely what those were. When the Russians sent their cosmonaut Yuri Gagarin into space for the first time 3 years later, on April 12, 1961, they sincerely thought that the Americans were left much behind in the race. The

Russians were proved wrong. In another 8 years thereafter, the Americans could make a human walk on the moon for the first time as a befitting response to the USSR! Neil Armstrong made the 'Giant Leap for Mankind' on July 20, 1969, as we all know.

Slightly bigger than a basketball, with whisker-like features of a cat as an antenna, it was the launch of 'Sputnik 1' by Russia (erstwhile USSR) - not the US - that opened the doors of the space age, heralding the space race and space explorations which continue to this day. Remarkably, this war took place during my time and many more players have joined since then - France, Germany, the UK, Japan, China, India, and more. Definitely, this topic would not have come to my mind if India had not made the mission Chandrayaan 3, becoming the first country to soft-land a satellite successfully recently on the southern polar region of the moon. I am trying to take stock of how this that race had started historically rather than scientifically, especially for the reading of youngsters and old-timers alike, including my granddaughters Maria and Serah, who will understand well later, if not now, a must-read.

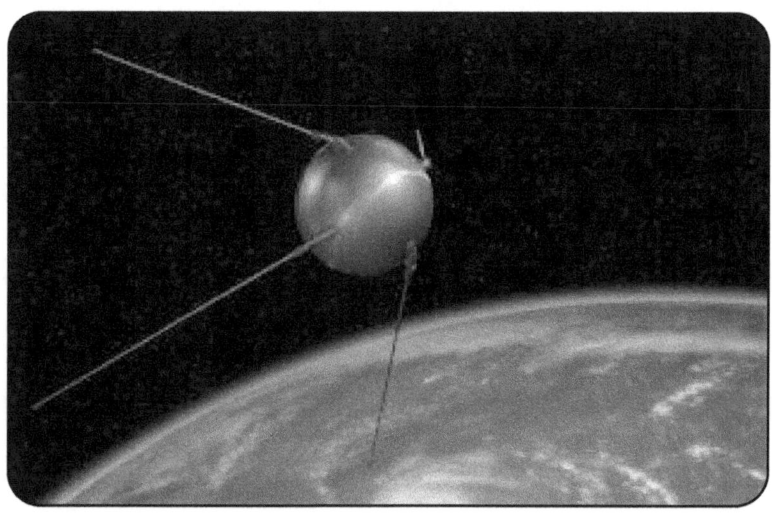

Development of Science in the US and Russia (USSR)

In spite of the fact that at least 8 Founding Fathers of the US, including Benjamin Franklin and Thomas Jefferson, were renowned scientists, most of Europe was much more advanced in scientific explorations comparatively until almost the mid-20th century.

Russia's history of scientific development started from the Czarist days. Peter the Great established the Imperial Academy of Sciences as early as 1725. By 1917, when the Communists came to power, that country already had 4 fully-fledged universities. The USSR gave much importance to Mathematics, Nuclear Science, and Astronomy thereafter, churning out thousands of Scientists and Engineers, much more than relative to the world population then.

But all these actions did not bring the standards in Russia either to what was available, notably in Britain and Germany, because of the long-established scientific infrastructure, societies, universities, and institutes there over centuries. Then what made the US and Russia (USSR) lead the race of space explorations all of a sudden?

US, V2 and a Man from NAZI to NASA

Nazi Germany was much ahead in Quantum Physics and Rocket Science compared to any other country in the world. But Nazi thoughts of Hitler were not conducive for Jewish citizens who were leading the scientists in that country even to survive there. As the Nazis started their influence over Germany and Italy, there was a steady flow of Jewish German scientists to the US, which the latter encouraged. The famous Albert Einstein was one among those who migrated to the US in 1933, which was followed by many others. We all know how the US managed to have the first nuclear explosion with the help of such emigrants, including Oppenheimer, in 1944.

Nazi Germany was able to develop the first long-range guided ballistic missile, codenamed V2, much ahead of others. It was the brainchild of the Nazi German aerospace scientist Werner Von Braun and his team. V-2 was the world's first functional large-scale liquid propellant rocket which the Nazi army secretly developed at Peenemünde island in Germany. Just before the Red Army captured this island on May 5, 1945, Braun and his entire team of about 125 and about 1600 other German scientists had moved out secretly to surrender to US forces along with truckloads of related research papers. The secret US operation was codenamed as 'Paperclip.' No one knows the correct numbers.

The US was able to place Wernher Von Braun as Director of NASA (National Aeronautics and Space Administration). He was on the cover of many American publications later, including Life magazine! The fact that he became a US citizen and was regarded as the 'Father of Rocket Science' in that country was never an accident! The Redstone missile, which made Alan Shepard possible as the first US astronaut to travel into space in 1971, was a direct derivative of V-2!

At the same time, I don't think that US Science was any substandard before the Germans reached there. But they took advantage of the situation before and after WW2, which definitely gave an impetus to the scientific society there. Since the 1950s to this day, Americans have won half of the Nobel prizes awarded in Sciences, which is a world record yet to be broken! When the Electronics, Medicine, and IT boom started too, Americans were the leaders for sure.

German Scientists picked up in Operation Paperclip in US-1946.

V2, Forerunner of all ballistic missiles, developed by Nazi Germany.

Russia (USSR), ROSCOSMOS, V.2 and Nazi Germany

Russia was fully aware of Braun and V-2. But they couldn't stop him and the team of 125 from going to the US as they preferred to surrender to them, though it was the Red Army which reached Berlin first on May 2, 1945, with access to the Reichstag and Hitler's dwelling. Russians did the best of the next available options. They took the V-2 assembly facility at Peenemünde to bits to decipher their workings, along with detailed drawings and shipped available data to Moscow! Americans and the British had to wait another 2 months until July 4, 1945, to have an entry to Berlin. But they had their pieces of cake from elsewhere in Germany!

ROSCOSMOS is the equivalent of NASA in Russia if you don't know. Under 'Operation Osoaviakhim', Russians identified about 2500 Nazi German scientists - altogether 6500 including family members - who were transferred to the Soviet Union, latest by October 22, 1946, in 92 trains! The famous rocket engineer Helmut Grottrup, who was a colleague of Braun, was one among them. He, along with other Germans such as Johannes Hoch, Kurt Mogus etc., have contributed German technology to the USSR. Here I have to mention that Grotropp defected to West Germany in 1953 and invented the first smart card in the world thereafter! Americans exploded the first atomic bomb in 1944, but Russians followed suit in 1949, now you know how! The famous rocket of the USSR codenamed R-5M, was made on the basis of V-2, as seen below.

Soviets in Berlin hoisting their flag over Reichstag

V-2 and India

V of V-2 stands for a difficult German word to pronounce for me- 'Vergetltungswaffezweir', which means 'Vengeance Weapon'. It is estimated that thousands of concentration slave workers had perished in manufacturing them by Nazis. Nevertheless, both countries- America and Russia - considered V-2 as an antecedent of their own ballistic missiles and space launch vehicles and used effectively related German scientists. It is a true record of history that even those countries don't deny! When the US and the West used to look down on India while getting onto the bandwagon of the atomic club or aerospace club with our own humble but honest efforts with all our problems, including poverty, I never knew that they had such a negative past! And I don't think that most of my fellow Indians either. Perhaps even those who live in the West now also may not be fully aware, as only after the Cold War was over it is known in the public domain. But look at the double standards of the western outlook! They laugh at us, forgetting what they did in this field with the Nazis.

The cartoon was published in NYT when India sent a record number of satellites in a day. They later apologised for the same. Given another opportunity, they may probably repeat!

In 1925, almost 100 years back, a US cartoon predicted that one day, the balance of power would shift!

Always remember that the great invention of 'zero' ('sunya' in Sanskrit) by Indian Mathematicians in the 5th century was more than nothing. That's why Albert Einstein himself said once: "We owe a lot to Indians, who taught us to count, without which no worthwhile scientific discovery could have been made". Intelligent Westerners like Max Muller, Mark Twain, Romain

Rolland, and Will Durant, the list can be longer, have testified similar accounts if you require such consolations from the West itself. But I also remember that we cannot live quoting our glorious past alone.

India is a very young country in the quest for aerospace adventures compared to existing experts. But the new economic situation of the country, making it one of the richest in GDP, has opened many avenues for the country and countrymen. And the situation will be much better as the years go by. We may not have Godfathers to help us or need not be copycats as the West did, but still, I feel that in the next 25 years, India will turn around to be a fully blossomed, robust nation in this respect. All we do is inject a sense of nationalism in the veins of Indian youngsters, giving professional opportunities to grow in our own country, who now make serpentine queues in front of the US and other western consulates to immigrate! Make them understand that after scoring excellent grades from the best institutes in the country, which are on par with the best in the world in Sciences and Engineering, do not settle for selling FMCG or beauty products or cool drinks here or abroad just for the sake of some more monies to earn! Sure, there is nothing wrong with those careers, but they are making others lose chances to enter and study Science and engineering in such prestigious colleges of fame and become world-class Scientists and Engineers! Let us resolve the problem of poverty in India also, along with becoming a super powerhouse in Science, Technology and Economy- not forgetting Arts, Literature, Humanities and others- reminding the fact that Science can help it be accomplished more than anything else! We have to grow ourselves and protect ourselves! We have the right capabilities. We have to make it happen.

I shall sign off here after making 2 cartoons as above. The first one could be a repeat for you. Elite Space Club of the US/Europe made fun of India when the latter shot more than a hundred satellites in one go, a world record so far. The second is to show that all Westerners are not fools. One of them had made a cartoon about 100 years back forecasting what India would do now and in future! US cartoonist Bob Minor published in 1925 a prediction that one day, the balance of power would shift to China, India, and Africa! I don't think that even an Indian could dream of such a status for India at that time.

Definitely, I may not live long enough to see this situation happen. But that is secondary.

FROM THE DIARY OF A BRITISH SURGEON WHO MADE 'PASSAGE TO INDIA' EASIER!

The more I read about the history of India, especially how the British East India Company (EIC) came to power and colonised the country, the more intricate and convoluted it became to me. New unknown names and characters come to the central stage all of a sudden from nowhere, which the Indian historians have hardly mentioned, for reasons beyond my comprehension!

Such a name is Dr. William Hamilton, a surgeon who came to India in 1717. How come a doctor played a crucial and decisive role in the affairs of EIC, which ultimately captured the control of India? Such a reflection can still be seen on the grave inscriptions of the doctor at St John's Church, Calcutta, which is given below. It ends with 'he made his own name famous at the court of the Great Monarch, and without a doubt, will perpetuate his memory as well in Great Britain as all other nations of Europe.'

Here is another episode on how Britain became 'great' at the expense of the oppression of Indians and systematic looting of resources for centuries, one of the biggest benefactors of his country. How did EIC become the bellwether of the British Economy? What are the roles of surgeons in the establishment of the domain of EIC in India? at least in one instance, EIC reps were forced to prostrate in front of the Indian emperor, asking for forgiveness in a child's war.

EIC Coat of Arms

1600 EIC Is Born

It was in the year 1600 that Queen Elizabeth I of Britain granted a petition signed by over 200 merchants of London, allowing them to trade with the Eastern world. Thus, East India Company (EIC) was formed on 31 December 1600, making it the first joint stock company in the world. It was during the reign of Akbar, the Mughal emperor in India, that this incident happened, which was hardly noticed in many parts of even Britain or Europe, forget about India. After all, having a trading relationship with India existed from time immemorial by Romans, Phoenicians, Greeks, Venetians, Egyptians, Chinese, and Arabs. 'Red Dragon', the first ship owned by EIC, set sail to the East Indies (Indonesia) under the command of James Lancaster soon. Medical Officers were employed as ship surgeons who were qualified to treat the crew of the ships initially and later the staff of EIC at shores as they were not sure of the quality of medical service available on

the lands they would trade.

'Red Dragon' Docks in India - The First EIC Factory

It was in 1612 that the 'Red Dragon' came to India for the first time, which was under the command of Thomas Best, who could get trading rights at Surat. In 1613, the first EIC factory in India was established there. Gabriel Boughton, the ship's surgeon, is said to have saved Princess Jahanara, daughter of the reigning Mughal emperor Shah Jehan, from injuries due to burns. The emperor was pleased, and the incident acted as a catalyst for giving trading rights and eventually awarding duty-free rights to EIC. By 1647, EIC had 23 factories in India. Money started pouring into London in leaps and bounds, in spite of a few Anglo-Dutch wars!

Initial Humiliating Setback for EIC: Child's War

When it was thought that everything was in order for a thriving business in India, the relationships with the Mughal Emperor Aurangzeb soured. In 1689, a Mughal fleet under the command of Sidi Yaqut defeated the forces of EIC at Bombay when Sir Josiah Child was their governor in London. The company was forced to seek pardon from the emperor by sending their representatives to prostrate in front of the emperor for forgiveness. I don't think EIC had to do such an act before or after in the history of India! And I wonder why I did not know that all these years!

Soon after, the company decided to concentrate on Calcutta to continue the business.

William Hamilton's Role Commences

He reached India as a surgeon on the ship named 'Sherborne'. Later, he was appointed as the second surgeon to the British settlement in India in 1711. When the British Embassy started operation at Calcutta in 1714, he was reappointed as medical officer.

It was Farrukhsiyar, the tenth Mughal ruler, who reigned in north India between 1713 and 1719. He also happened to be Aurangzeb's great-grandson, who came to power after assassinating his own uncle. He was a handsome man but lacked the brightness to rule his kingdom on his own, depending on his advisers!

In 1715, EIC decided to send a delegation to the emperor at Delhi to ask for major grants for the further establishment of the company affairs in India. They were mainly (1) to purchase 38 villages surrounding the headquarters of the company in Bengal, (2) Trading privileges in Bengal, and (3) further fortifications of Calcutta. Why EIC decided to include William Hamilton, who is a medical officer at the Embassy, in such a delegation is not known. It could be that they remembered the services of Gabriel Doughton in 1613 or might have heard about the decease the emperor had, which was kept as a state secret.

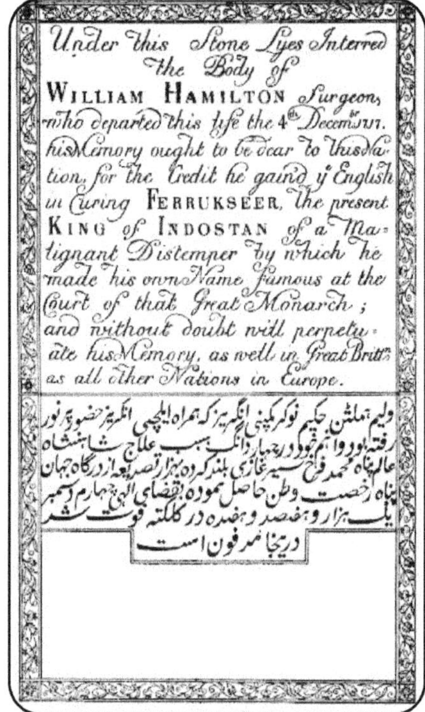

How William Hamilton succeeds in getting the grants 'Magna Carta' of EIC leading to British Raj!

Farrukhsiyar's second marriage was fixed with Princess Indira Kanwar, daughter of Maharaja Ajit Singh, Rajput of Jodhpur. The conquered Rajput king wanted to make a treaty with the Mughals by submission to Delhi. But the marriage had to be postponed many times due to a very bad ailment the emperor had on his groins. He had a bad swelling there and no indigenous medicines of Vydhyas and Hakims were effective. That's when William Hamilton reached Delhi and was consulted by the emperor. The surgeon took a chance and made an operation which was successful. Needless to note that the emperor was more than pleased!

The surgeon was honoured by gifting a lot of valuables, including an elephant! But the unexpected bonanza was for the East India Company as the emperor sanctioned the requests of the company in full, issuing a Farman! This, in hindsight, turned out to be the 'Magna Carta' of EIC, eventually making the company loot India high and dry!

After the grant, Farrukhsiyar expressed his wish to retain the surgeon at Delhi, but Hamilton refused. Dr. Hamilton died in 1717 at Calcutta, the same year of the grant, while Farrukhsiyar was assassinated in 1719 at Delhi! EIC played the right trump card at the right time.

GENGHIS KHAN WAS NOT A 'KHAN'

For all of us, the very name of Genghis Khan brings the chill of a cruel conqueror of the past. He could be one of the cruellest of all. Having his empire centred in Mongolia, he conquered and ruled all the lands between the Pacific Ocean and the Caspian Sea – a historic fact. Like the Mughals - a term derived from 'Mongol' in Persian language - emperors who originated from those areas much later, almost all of us believe that he too was a Muslim emperor. But he was not. He was not a Muslim at all, though his surname was Khan! He belonged to a Turkish Mongol culture which worshipped Tengri, a mountain God! I am sure that you have not heard of Tengrism either. He was instrumental in killing millions of humans as his army advanced to occupy foreign lands, but interestingly, he was tolerant of all religions in the new territories he had conquered! Like Alexander the Great, Genghis Khan also left India untouched although he had reached Delhi and could defeat the ruler easily, for unknown reasons.

He had asked his fellows to bury his body in secret, which they did upon his death in 1227. To this day, nobody knows or could find that location despite many renowned historians and professionals having tried to find the spot. Even the latest satellite imagery and related techniques have not been fruitful in finding out his burial place, where a large treasure is also expected to be found! Here is Genghis Khan you didn't know.

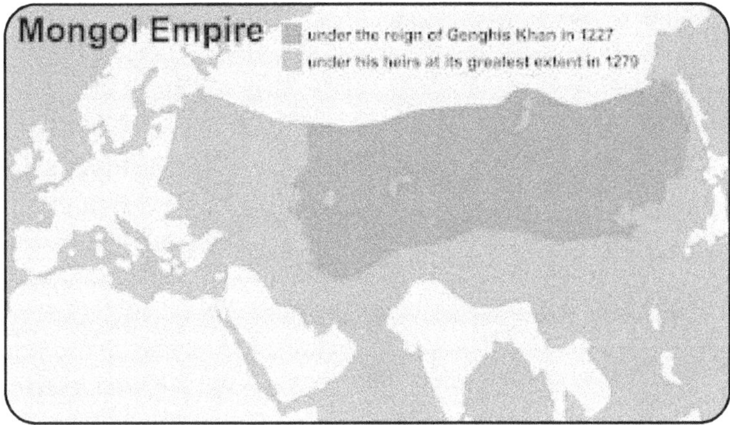

Temujin to Genghis Khan

His original name was Tejumin, and he was a warrior with insignificant beginnings. Initially, within a few years, he brought all the nomadic tribes of Mongolia under him. Then he started his plunderous conquests of the near and far, establishing his Mongolian empire, which spread to China, the Middle East, Korea, Japan, and Eastern Europe! Genghis Khan made himself a 'khan', meaning a great ruler. He adapted his name, Genghis Khan, meaning universal ruler! He ruled between 1206-1227.

<u>What Made Him A Successful Conqueror?</u>

He was ruthless with his enemies, which could be the first. Mongol military tactics and organisations were the main factors, which enabled them to conquer foreign lands to the extent of establishing the largest land empire in the history of mankind! His army men were expert archers, extremely tough, and could ride horses for days with minimal food and water. The primary weapon was bows with which they could fire arrows double the distance of their competing armies. His ministers and commanders came from 20 different nations, many of whom were his enemies earlier who had surrendered to him. This also shows that he had a mastermind. The father of Genghis Khan was killed by his rivals by poisoning during his sleep. In order to ward off such incidents in his own life, Genghis Khan raised a special force named Keshik who were his bodyguards during day and night. They were well paid, well looked after, and outranked any others in his army. They were an elite class. Mughal emperors in India had palace soldiers of the same name, Keshik, which could be news to you.

Monument erected for Genghis Khan in Mongolia

Ruthlessness and Burial

It is estimated that 40 million or more people might have been killed due to the adventures of Genghis Khan, which accounts for 10% of the world's population at that time! Most of them were innocent! While he was extremely cruel on one side, he was tolerant of all religions in the countries he had conquered. Christians, Buddhists, and Muslims were all given religious freedom to practice and were even exempted from tax for places of worship.

He had instructed his followers to bury his body in secret, which they did upon his death on 18 August 1227 from an unknown illness. Nobody knows exactly where he was buried.

Tengrism

Genghis Khan practised the religion of Tengrism, which is an ethnic Mongolic Trlic religion. They have a sky God, Tengri, and related natural aspects of the world such as earth, water, fire, the sun, the moon, storms, rainbow and the like. Tengrism is still practised by a few in Mongolia and elsewhere. Genghis Khan brought the spoken language of the Mongol into a written one. A uniform civil code was established during his tenure and implemented in all the lands he ruled. A new postal system, where horse-riding couriers carried messages, was set up. He is revered as a godlike figure in the region even now and respected as the Father of Mongolia.

GUILLOTINE: HOW A KILLING MACHINE BECAME A SYMBOL OF EQUALITY

While the French Revolution gave the world 'Liberty, Equality, and Fraternity', which reverberated throughout the world, though not necessarily immediately like in India, it also gave a killing tool some sort of status in French society! The guillotine, which was promoted by a surgeon, became respectable at that time since it symbolised equality in death as well! When it was introduced in 1789 by Dr. Joseph Ignace Guillotin as a lawmaker, this was the logic behind it, and the name of the equipment became associated with his family name. Until capital punishment was stopped recently in France in 1981, the guillotine continued to be used.

As the guillotine way of execution, which was quick and considered to be more humane compared to the various methods of execution that existed until then, King Louis XVI was slaughtered in public in 1793, declaring the country to be a republic, followed by Queen Marie Antoinette in the same year! During the days of the 'Reign of Terror' (1793-94), fights among revolutionaries themselves following the execution of the king took place, while the Jacobins eventually took control. 40,000 such executions took place using guillotines, executions that were popular among the masses as entertainment and were staged in public.

How The Guillotine Came into France

The story of beheading was different around the world. At least 500 years before the guillotine was put into practice in France, similar but cruder methods of execution existed in Ireland, Italy, and England. The "Planke" of Germany, the Scottish "Maiden," and the "Mannaia" of Italy are some of them. The "Halifax Gibbet" was used in England in the 12th century. In 1790, Dr. Joseph Ignace Guillotin did not invent the machine, but as a lawmaker, he promoted the idea that the death penalty should be equal for all regardless of the crimes committed or the social ranking of the person who committed them! In fact, this machine was invented by another surgeon, Antoine Louis. Initially, the machine was called the Louisette. Dr. Guillotin presented his 6 articles as follows and they became law in France:

1. Offences of the same kind will be punished by the same kind of penalty.

2. In all cases where the law imposes the death penalty on an accused person, the punishment shall be the same, regardless of the nature of the offence of which he is guilty; the criminal shall be decapitated; this will be done solely by means of a simple mechanism.

3. In view of the personal character of the crime, no punishment of a guilty person shall involve any discredit to his family. The honour of those belonging to him shall not be soiled in any way, and they shall continue to be admissible to any kind of profession, employment, and public function.

4. No one shall reproach a citizen with any punishment imposed on one of his relatives. Whoever ventures to do so shall be publicly reprimanded by the judge. The sentence imposed on him shall be written on the offender's door. Moreover, it shall be displayed on the pillory and remain there for a period of 3 months.

5. Confiscation of the condemned person's property shall not be imposed in any case.

6. The corpse of an executed man shall be handed over to his family upon their request. In every case, he shall be allowed a normal burial, and no reference shall be made on the register to the nature of his death. Unquote.

The Machine

The device releases a sharp blade from a height of 226 centimetres. With the combined weight of the blade and counterweight, the guillotine can cut through the neck of a human being within 0.005 seconds! According to Guillotin, this invention was one of the best outcomes of the revolution - humane, equalising, and scientific! A guillotine blade that was originally used during the revolution for executions is exhibited in Paris at the Police Museum. Still, it remains a star attraction!

By the time Joseph Guillotin died at the age of 75, the machine had become synonymous with terror, with his family name attached to it. After his death, his relatives approached the government to change the name of the machine, but their request was rejected. It could be a paradox in history that instead the family changed the name!

Earrings and Tricoteuses of the Revolutionary Period

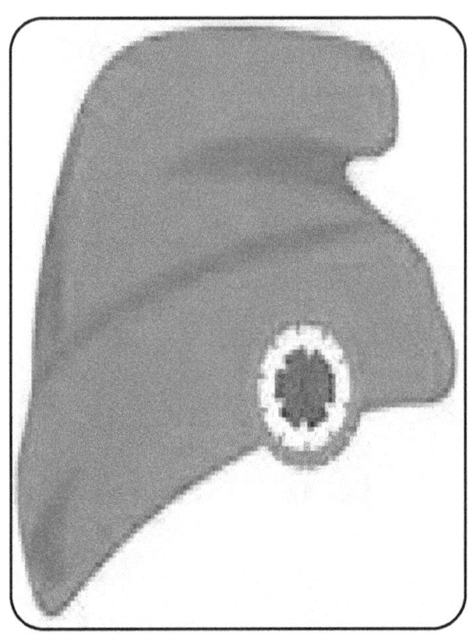

Tricoteuses is a French term used to describe 'a knitting woman' who used to flock in thousands to watch live executions staged in public while continuing to knit! It became a nickname to describe the women who sat to watch the executions by guillotine and coolly knit, enjoying the spectacle! The liberty cap they knit in those days became infamously popular. Charles Dickens, in his famous novel 'A Tale of Two Cities', has popularised the images of Tricoteuses extensively. Even fashion was influenced by earrings modelled after the guillotine, as seen above.

Ironically, Hitler made the guillotine the state method of execution in the 1930s and 40s, with 20 such machines placed across German cities, killing thousands!

Tailpiece: The Cross

Having written about the guillotine and how it was regarded as a symbol of equality in death in modern society, in France and elsewhere, if I skipped over a killing device which has arguably become the most popular in world history, I would be unfair. The Cross, the most important symbol of Christianity, not only remains a symbol of hope and peace but also has been revered among Christians for the last 2000 years!

HEAVENLY FRAGRANCE OF GODS WAS FROM INDIA

Happy New Year to all my readers worldwide! Let me kick off the new edition of the new year with a hardly known historical fact about India.

It is a fact that despite our resources and local demand, India doesn't produce many consumer goods of Indian origin. Most of the FMCG items we manufacture and use are international brands, though made in India. But steadily, the scenario is changing, I notice, and in the next 10 years, India could change the current speed of it, I am sure.

In the field of cosmetics and perfumes, we are nowhere, though the consumption rate has gone high. Parisian brands are the most sought-after here, too for those who can afford it. I have read somewhere that the famous Indian brand in that field, 'Lakme,' was started by Tata's Unilever at the request of our first Prime Minister Nehru to JRD Tata to create an Indian brand which our women could afford. JRD earnestly took the request, ending up in the creation of the brand 'Lakme'. But many of us may not be aware that 'Lakme' is a French rendition of the Sanskrit word 'Lakshmi', who is the Goddess of wealth and beauty in Hinduism. Though Lakme, created in 1952, has become a premier brand in India and is even exported to around 70 countries, now the House of Tatas represents and just distributes a lot of imported international brands in India through their enterprise Tata Luxury, even online! Maybe good for the organisation for profits but definitely not for the country. Just an observation and nothing more since I am not an expert in the field. It is comparable to our computer hardware field, where our own brands are much less, though we claim ourselves to be software giants!

But here I am to share a hardly known information among us that India has one of the richest histories in its own fragrances and perfumes, which is yet to be commercially tapped. Here I am writing about Agarwood or Aloes or Oud, a fragrance of Indian origin that has mastered the fragrance world since 1400 BC, about which I shamefully came to know first from Arabs only, while in Qatar.

Oud shops in Mumbai

It was Mr. Sherida Al Kaabi, chairman of the business group 'Al Balagh' where I had been working in Qatar, who first told me that among the Oud wood, the best and costliest comes from India! I specifically remember him mentioning this while we were strolling the Mumbai Fort area, looking for some specific shops selling them. We were on a business trip. To be very honest and frank, when I had landed in Qatar in 1984, I was so ignorant about perfumes and fragrances that I did not know the difference between an eau de cologne, eau de toilette, and eau de parfum! I didn't know about Oud wood chips either. I think many educated Indians could still be in that state even now.

But let us be awake, fellow Indians. We introduced the first, most popular fragrance to the rest of the world centuries ago. Whether in ancient Egypt, Greece, Rome, the Middle East, or elsewhere,

India has historically made it the 'favourite fragrance of the Gods', as mentioned in seminal texts of Hinduism, Judaism, Christianity, Buddhism, or Islam.

A Spiritual History Unfolds

Agarwood of Assam, India, and its mystifying fragrance were first mentioned in the Sanskrit epic 'Mahabharata' in 1500 BC. There it is referred to as a welcome aroma, 'Agaru'. The earliest recorded use of this plant aromatics is found in the 4 Vedas of ancient India, written between 1500-1000 BC. Similarly, in the Arthasastra of 320 BC, it is clearly mentioned that the aromatics originate from resin-infused infected wood in the stem of the Agar tree or even artificially done so! Agarwood has been used as an ingredient of perfumery in India along with sandalwood, musk, and camphor from ancient times. Hindus have burnt incense sticks in puja rooms and elsewhere from time immemorial. It is known as 'Agarbatti', derived from 'Agar bathi' in Hindi - an incense stick made from Agarwood!

In the Old Testament of the Bible, Aloe (Agaru) is specifically mentioned many times, perhaps because it was in use in Jewish traditions. Even in the New Testament, as per the Gospel of John 19:39-40, it is stated that Jesus's body was anointed with a mixture of Myrrh and Aloes following His crucifixion!

In 'Nirvana Sutra Buddhism', when Buddha was about to enter the state of Nirvana, there is a mention of Aloe aromatics. Buddhist text 'Jataka Tales' of the 4th century BC also mentions Aloe categorically!

Pre-Islamic Arabian tribes were trading in Aloeswood/Agarwood in India. In the Quran, there is a mention of many fragrant plants. In several Hadiths, Oud (Agarwood) is referred to as an Indian Incense for rituals, such as the burning of incense wood, which is being practised in many Islamic countries to this day.

Since I am not an expert on holy books, all as these references are made from historical records available and any wrong interpretations are to be taken in that spirit.

Black Gold

Botanically, when an Agar tree - Aquilaria Malaccensis - becomes infected by a mould - Phialophora Parasitica - the tree produces a dark, dense, and fragrant resin to protect itself. It is this resin which becomes embedded in the tree, which is the source of Oud! As in the case of a pearl, such resin can also be produced artificially. Originally discovered in India in Assam, locally known as Xasi, the 'info and technique' of Agarwood was later passed on to Tibet (a-ga-ru), China (Chen Xiang), Thailand (Mai Krishna), South East Asia, and the Middle East, where it was known as Oud.

As the nouveau riche of the Arabian Gulf states, like fragrances and perfumes, the area became a big market for this costly oil - more than $12,000 per kg! International brands of perfumes from Paris and London vie with each other for their market share with new fragrances in new bottles at new prices each season - the highest-ever perfume created for a human nose so far! From Tom Ford to Christian Dior to Armani or Yves Saint Laurent. However, the fact remains that this fragrance is not popular among Westerners.

It all started in India centuries ago. It is high time that Indians take note of it! Not only do we have to teach others, but we also have to learn from others - what we don't know or are not good at. It is difficult to believe that now India produces one of the best whiskies in the world, surpassing even renowned Scotch brands - 'Amrut' single malt. And the best cheese in the world, surpassing all the best European brands - 'Eleftheria Brunost', is from Bombay! I am sure that among perfumes also, we are capable of competing with Paris - just a matter of time.

<u>Tailpiece:</u>

I don't find any mention of this history in Indian textbooks! I wish that I was wrong.

Dr. Rajan Varghese, Ex-Principal of UC College, has shared the following postal stamps of India on the subject. His comments are given in the appropriate column.

"I CAN" IS 100 TIMES MORE IMPORTANT THAN "I.Q"

What's common with Albert Einstein, Leonardo da Vinci and Stephen W Hawking? High rate of intelligence, of course. They were not known to be subjected to IQ tests in their lifetime, though.IQ stands for Intelligence Quotient, as we all know. The intelligence of any individual is difficult to measure, it is said. Yet, this has not stopped us from getting attracted by intelligence tests.

What's the score for an average IQ rating? What score would the above gentlemen have scored in such tests, or to put it another way, how much is given to them each by the scientific community? Which community or countrymen top the list with the highest IQ rating in the world? Being an Indian, I was curious to know where an average Indian stands on the scale.

The biggest irony is that the first IQ test ever Invented by 2 professional psychologists from France in 1905 was not to find out the brightest among students, but on the contrary, the weakest who may require support in their studies. Read about IQ, the most sought-after 'commodity' in the world, of which most of us are not aware!

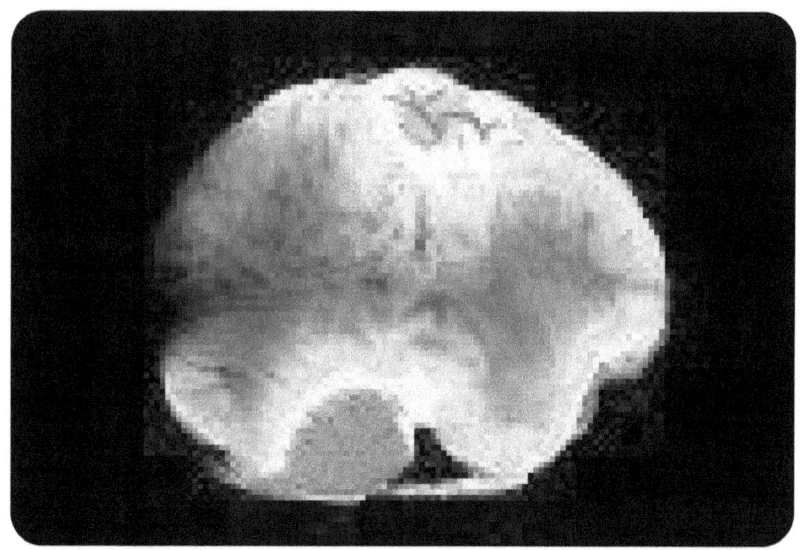

The First IQ Test

It was in 1905 that 2 French Psychologists named Alfred Binet and Theodore Simon designed a professional IQ test for children. It was never known as an IQ test then because the abbreviation IQ was coined by a German Psychologist named William Stern only in 1912. The intention of Binet and Simon in formulating the test was for schoolchildren to identify those who are struggling in their studies so that they can be supported! But it so happened that this test became the basis of all modern IQ tests which came thereafter to this day!

Salient Ratings Of IQ Tests

Most people, when tested, fall between 85 and 115, while 100 is considered average. It is found that career-wise, the IQ ratings of Managers and Administrators are lower than those of professional doctors and technocrats. Salespeople stand even lower!

What about sex differences in intelligence? Test results show that in certain test batteries, males perform better, while in others, females do. In overall performance, there is zero difference. It is also found that among races, there is no variation! It has also been proven that the new generation fares better than the old because of better education, better nutrition, and better environments.

The Dark History of Tests

All countries have an imperfect history, and the US and others are no exceptions. While Adolf Hitler is notoriously projected as the champion of racism practised at its extreme in the world, do you know about the Virginia Sterilisation Act of 1924, which allowed sterilisation of the feebleminded in the US? Similarly, in Nordic countries like Denmark, Finland, Norway, and Sweden in the 1930s.

A poster in the US by those who believed in Eugenics!

Based on Eugenics - the practice of selective breeding of the human population based on IQ tests - there was definitely a dark past in the history of mankind concerning such tests. It was as late as 2001 that the Virginia General Assembly passed a joint resolution expressing regret over such incidents and offered compensation to the victims, expected to be not less than 7000!

During WWI, the US Army used to conduct 2 types of tests for new recruits, named as Alpha and Beta tests, it is recorded. The first was a written test, while the second was for those who couldn't read.

However, thankfully, the intentions and practices of IQ tests, which are based on verbal reasoning, working memory, and visual-spatial skills, have improved all around the world over the years.

Countries On Top of the list in IQ Rating

The best 10 countries in the world in IQ rankings are as below:

1. Japan   106.48

2. Taiwan   106.47

3. Singapore   105.89

4. Hong Kong (China)   105.37

5. China   104.10

6. South Korea   102.35

7. Belarus   101.60

8. Finland   101.20

9. Liechtenstein   101.70

10. Germany &Netherlands   100.74

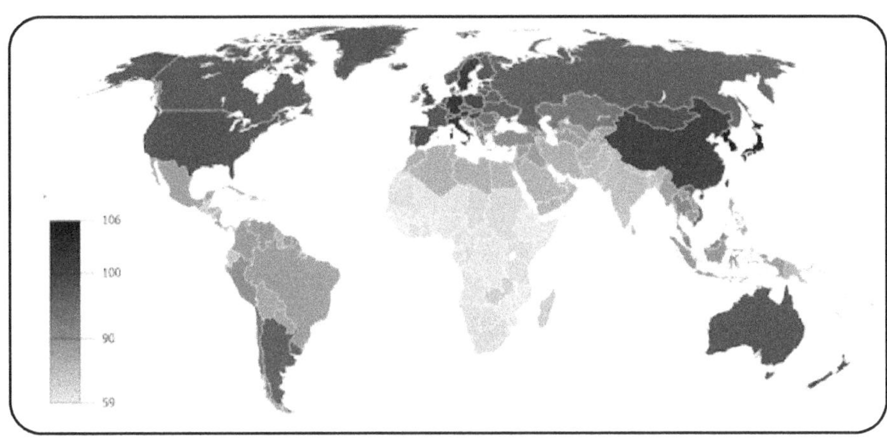

One can notice that there is hardly any difference in scores between the first and second, which are Japan and Taiwan! Also, one can notice that the first 6 countries are from Asia and from one region more or less. In spite of this fact, the Europeans made Asia their colonies and stole all our resources. Still, they do in one way or another. I have noticed that some surveys vary in results of the rankings but only in minor nature. Surprisingly - at least for me - India stands in a position of 143 only out of 199 countries. Unfortunately, India gets lower rankings in almost all the international ranking scales such as Hunger Index, Cleanliness, Pollution etc., in spite of being one of the richest countries in the world currently. The main reason could be the huge disparity in everything among the people, but in another 10 years, I think India will do much better.

Mensa International and TNS

There are a few international clubs/societies where membership is restricted to those with very high IQ ratings. Mensa International is such an organisation, having 134,000 members in 100 countries worldwide. Their requirement for membership is a score over the 98th percentile on certain standard IQ tests!

Another similar organisation is the Triple Nine Society or TNS. Their requirement for membership is the 99.9th percentile, as indicated in the name!

Tail Piece

While reading and writing a lot about these blessed people with a lot of intelligence, I find solace in the words of Socrates and Samuel Goldwyn. Socrates, we all know about. Samuel Goldwyn was a poor Polish Jew who migrated to the US and eventually became a leading businessperson apart from being a film producer and director there.

Socrates, who lived between 470 and 399 BC, philosophically stated, "I know that I am intelligent because I know nothing!" Samuel Goldwyn (1879-1974) was more practical when he concluded, "Give me a smart idiot over a stupid genius any day"! Albert Einstein himself has commented that "I can' is 100 times more important than "I.Q."

IN EUROPE, PINEAPPLE WAS "PINA DE INDES," "PINE OF THE INDIANS," A STATUS SYMBOL

Kerala, my home state in India, is blessed with a lot of locally grown tropical fruits. Pineapple is one among them. This exotic fruit is so cheap here that it is available for less than half a USD per KG! And it is abundantly available during the season. But when I read somewhere, that pineapple was a status symbol among the elite in Europe some time back— in the 16th and 17th centuries— I decided to make a trail of it to have a better understanding of the theme.

Pineapple is a native of South America, especially Brazil and Paraguay. It was known as 'Ananas Comosus' in Guarani, a local live language which existed there from the days of the conquest of the Spanish. It was Christopher Columbus in 1496 who brought a lone pineapple which survived his long voyage of weeks— in a ship which had only wind power— from the Caribbean island of Guadeloupe to Spain. He presented it to King Ferdinand as "pina de Indes"— the Pine of the Indians, thinking that he had just discovered India for this island! The king fell for the taste of the fruit, which was unknown to anyone in Europe till then! The heyday of pineapple commenced that day!

As pineapples started being available in a limited way in Europe, the wealthy went wild with the taste of this fruit.

Along with the taste, the pineapple became synonymous with nobility and wealth as it became the favourite of Charles II of Scotland, Catherine the Great of Russia, Louis XV of France and King Ferdinand of Spain!

From the Mayas to the "Pineries" of Europe

Around 750 BC, the Mayas and Aztecs of Mexico were the oldest civilisation to cultivate pineapples. Soon, it might have spread around the areas of that continent, but nothing was recorded until Christopher Columbus transported the first pineapple to Europe in 1496, which he named "pina de Indes"— the Pine of India. Just 25 years later, Magellan also discovered the pineapple plant in his exploration of Brazil. Spaniards named the fruit "pinas" due to its resemblance to a pine cone. In Europe, by the mid-1600s, pineapples were successfully cultivated in specially designed hothouses called "pineries". In 1677, the first European-grown pineapple in England was presented to King Charles II, and soon, the "pinery" became a status symbol.

Pineapple Madness

As the pineapple became sought-after, rivalries broke out among the aristocratic families of Europe! It was so expensive that only a few could afford to eat it. At one stage, it was "rented" out to banquets for display! Pineapples were carved into stones, carpets, sand, and wood by artists, making pineapple a luxury. By the 18th century, the fruit became an architectural feature of select buildings. In Europe, such a craze reverberated to the extent that a single fruit cost $8000 by today's standards!

How did the price come down?

By the early 18th century, steamships came into existence for navigation. Long voyages could be made in rather short periods, unlike the earlier ships, which depended on wind power. Transport of pineapples in bulk could also be facilitated in a shorter period, which made Europe get fresh supplies from faraway countries that were colonised by then. Pineapple became a product of the colony, and prices came down!

Similarly, many countries of South America saw pineapple cultivation flourish. In 1888, John L Jensen, a new migrant to the US, established a modern plantation of 133 acres and an export centre in Florida. In 1899, James D Dole, a Harvard graduate, developed a modern pineapple plantation of 65 acres in Hawaii, earning him the nickname "pineapple king"!

Now

As the scientific world found out that pineapples are low in calories while high in vitamins, minerals, and antioxidants, the fruit— fresh as well as canned— has become very popular. The largest producers of pineapples currently are the Philippines, Costa Rica, and Brazil. Even fresh pineapples come under world-renowned brands like Del Monte, Dole, and Chiquita. The best and tastiest pineapple is the Caribbean Antigua Black pineapple, although it is not black.

Pineapple cultivation was introduced to India in 1548 by Portuguese colonists in Kerala and Goa but was limited to traditional cultivation. Assam, Meghalaya, and Tripura are the states where pineapples are largely grown in India currently. There is a village named Vazhakulam near my hometown, which is very well-known for this exotic fruit and, I believe, has a geographical tag for taste and quality. I read the other day that Kerala state is in the process of making wine from locally grown pineapples and a few more fruits.

I am sure that only a few might have observed pineapple motifs built on the famous Charminar at Hyderabad, as seen below. Interestingly, it has been there since the 16th century built by the Qutb Shahi dynasty.

To this day, when the best hotels and banquet halls display fruits from all over the world, they will be crowned with a fresh pineapple! Many countries of the world call pineapple as ananas to this day, especially those who speak Arabic, Hindi, German, French, and Greek. This is the story of Pina de Indes or ananas—oops—pineapple!

INDIA'S LAKE OF SKELETONS

Skeleton Lake? In India? That was my initial reaction upon learning about this lake. Roopkund, a glacier lake containing hundreds of human skeletons, is situated in the Himalayas.

In fact, this lake, housing hundreds of skeletons, lies in the slopes of the Trishul massif, a mountain range in the Himalayas, about which I was equally uninformed, much like with Skeleton Lake.

Trishul I, Trishul II, and Trishul III are 3 mountains grouped in the Himalayas, collectively known as Trishula. This trio of peaks resembles a trident! Trisula, in Sanskrit, refers to a trident, believed to be the weapon of Lord Shiva by Hindus, while the Himalayas are considered his abode.

Skelton Lake and Trishula I, II and III

Discovery

At an altitude of 5000 metres, the area around the lake is uninhabited and can be reached in the State of Uttarakhand, possibly only by mountaineers. When the water level shrinks and is not frozen, the skulls and bones can be seen for one or 2 months a year during summer.

In 1942, a Game Reserve Ranger named Hari Krishna Madhwal discovered the skeletons accidentally. Seeing hundreds of skeletons, it is reported that his assistants ran away initially! It was thought that the skeletons belonged to Japanese soldiers who tried to invade India during WWII, but upon detailed investigation by the British, it was confirmed that the bones were older than that period.

As late as 2004, a professional team from National Geographic magazine made an expedition to the lake and returned with 30 skeletons for their detailed studies. Some of the skeletons had hair and flesh attached to bones! DNA tests were conducted. It was finally confirmed that the skeletons were 1200 years old. Their death might have occurred in the 9th century AD!

In 2013, further studies were conducted, and the reason for the death of hundreds of people was found to be because of gigantic hailstorms, especially from the evidence on the bones of skulls and shoulders! Although the reason seems to be logical, the controversies are still on.

Some researchers are of the opinion that the skeletons belonged to a Hindu pilgrimage journey called Nanda Devi (a manifestation of Goddess Parvati) Raj Jot Yatra. The skeletons were of male-female groups belonging to a wide age range.

Roopkund Trek

In recent years, an organised trek by the Tourism Department, named as above, has been conducted during the favourable season. This trek is considered to be moderate to hard in terms of difficulty and is hailed as one of the most beautiful treks in India. The 53-kilometre trail passes through mountainous rivers, enthralling ridges, lush forests, and scenic meadows, typically divided into 6 days for completion starting from the base camp of Lohajung/Wan.

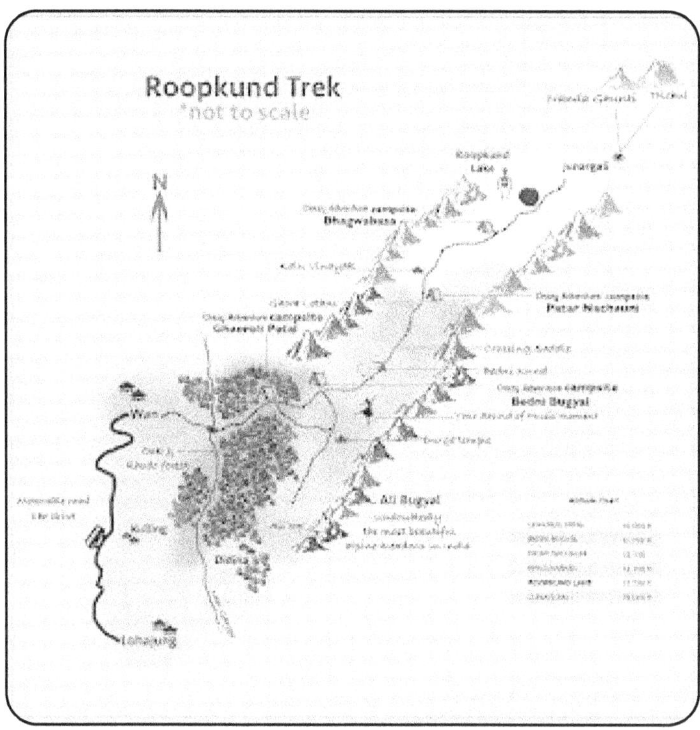

However, the government has reportedly banned such treks for the past 2 years due to concerns about disturbing the ecological systems of the area.

KILL EVERY BUFFALO (BISON) YOU CAN. EVERY BUFFALO DEAD IS AN INDIAN GONE! THANK GOD, HE MEANT NATIVE INDIAN OF THE US!

Human-wildlife conflict has been there in the annals of world history. Essentially, it is caused by competition for natural resources for existence by both parties, which is natural, more or less. But man was using his brains for the extermination of some species exclusively for his own gains, sometimes over another man, as happened in the US or out of ignorance or stupidity elsewhere.

Right from the days when wild animals like half-fed barbary lions or wine-fed bears were used to fight with gladiators Julius Caesar in the Colosseum of Rome for the amusement of people to these days when wild elephants and pigs forage on crops and tigers kill livestock in hilly regions of Kerala, and the local people clamour for action in my own state, this conflict is going on unabated.

Here, I shall showcase 3 cases where, in man's interest, the balance of nature and environments were compromised in modern times and its effects. "The Great Emu War" of Australia of 1932, China's Mao Zedong's "Four Pest Control" revolution in 1946 and "The Buffalo War of the US of the 1870s". The first was involved with killing Emus thousands, the very flightless bird which is still adored in Australia as depicted in their coat of arms. The second was killing millions of poor sparrows, among other creatures of nature, without knowing what they were doing really. Years later, China had to import thousands of sparrows from the Soviet Union, which is another truth. In the third case, the US was targeting the original inhabitants as well in the continent while hunting the bison in millions! Two kills with one bullet. Now, the US has identified bison as the national mammal!

Let me take up the last case first. Since then, the US and the West have advocated for 'Climate control, clean air, and environmental balance' for upcoming countries like India and China after doing everything possible on those topics for selfish interests.

The Bison War - US

In America, bison is commonly called buffalo by Americans. In the 18th and 19th centuries, a series of policies and events led to the near extinction of American bison. The main aim of European settlers was to weaken the Native American tribes since bison was a central resource for their food, clothing and shelter. This was a broader strategy of the US Govt and white settlers to force American Indians off their ancestral land and into reservations allocated for them. The ' bright' Europeans thought that this act would eventually kill the economies of Indians! And it did! The added advantage of the settlers was that they could also profit from the killings directly from bison meat and hides.

It was in 1872 that Colonel Richard Irving Dodge of the US Army made the famous (or infamous?) call to kill all buffalos possible, which I have used in the title! The new railroads even organised hunting excursions where passengers could shoot from the comforts of train carriages.

By 1868, in just 2 years, over 4 million buffalos were killed, while in 10 years thereafter, it reached a staggering figure of 30 million! Towards the end of the 19th century, the bison population, which had once numbered tens of millions in America, was reduced to a few hundred- one of the most severe cases of species depletion in human history.

The mountain is skulls of buffalos killed"

Once the settlers' aim was achieved, the government began conservation efforts. In 2016, the American bison was even declared the national mammal. I believe the story of the bison extends beyond wildlife conservation to encompass the policies adopted by the US government towards the Native American population.

The Four Pests Campaign - China

All of us know Mao Zedong's "Great Leap Forward" movement (1958-1962) in China. The "Four Pest Campaign" was part of this movement, targeting rats, flies, mosquitoes, and sparrows. Mao's campaign aimed to improve agricultural output and public health. Sparrows were included because they consumed a significant amount of grain, thus harming crop yields. Sparrows were systematically killed including their young ones. Eggs were broken. It was indeed a mass mobilisation campaign. Initially, the result was successful.

The mass killing of sparrows led to an ecological imbalance unexpectedly. The authorities failed to account for sparrows' role in controlling the population of insects which were harmful to crops. The lack of natural predators led to severe infestations. Famines followed by hardships!

After realising the utter folly, by 1958, the sparrow was spared for a new item- bed bug. But too late. The damage has already been done. It was a disaster for the ecosystem, and the greatest famine ever recorded in history happened in 1960, killing 45 million Chinese. But being a Communist country, one will never know. The authorities imported sparrows in thousands from many countries, including 250,000 Soviet Union.

The Great Emu War - Australia

The Emu War, while not a conventional conflict, could be described as a "nuisance wildlife management operation" that occurred in 1932. Following World War I, the Australian government allocated land to war veterans for farming in the region. These veterans were also offered subsidies to cultivate wheat in the newly allotted land. However, the government failed to anticipate the threat posed by emus to the crops.

The government declared an open attack on Emmu with the assistance of the Royal Australian Military, using even Lewis machine guns, which became famous in WWI. Thousands of Emmu retaliated against a military operation. In a few months, the operations had to be called off. The event is remembered for its absurdity.

MAN MAKES PLANS, GOD LAUGHS!

We all know the sad plight of the recent Ocean Gate expedition - to explore the wreckage of the sunken ship SS Titanic. In fact, for the last few decades, wealthy and adventurous tourists have been paying heavily to catch a glimpse of the wreck of the luxury ocean liner. This reminds me of a novel titled 'Futility' which I want to share with you. This spins around one John Rowald, who was in the US Navy but was dismissed from service due to alcoholism. To make a living, John joins a mighty British ocean liner called 'Titan' as a deck machinery assistant. The ship collides accidentally with a floating iceberg in the North Atlantic Sea. Then, only like others on the ship, John understands that the number of lifeboats arranged on the ship is much lower than what is actually required! The ship sinks to the bottom of the sea eventually!

Does this story remind you particularly of the actual story of 'The Titanic', the unsinkable ship? Yes, it does. But when you note that this novel "Futility" was first published in 1898, 14 years before 'The Titanic' was launched to sea in 1912, one will be surprised obviously.

What the American author of many short stories and novels named Morgan Robertson did was exactly that. The poor chap never made a claim to be astrologic when the Titanic hit the bottom of the Atlantic. He always thought that the actual wreck of the SS Titanic was just a coincidence to one of his stories! In spite of this creation, in fact, he failed to make a living as a professional writer until his death. Believe it, he had given an alternative title to this particular book-'The Wreck Of Titan', which is getting popular among readers these days! "Man makes plans, but God laughs" is a Yiddish proverb.

The 'Titan' and the 'Titanic' - Similarities That Cannot Be Ignored

The movie Titanic of 1997 is one of the all-time highest box office hits ever made. Based on the actual story of one of the worst but biggest shipwrecks we ever had, I am not going to elaborate on it once again since it is too well-known. Commencing the maiden journey from Southampton, UK, on April 10, 1912, the liner hit an iceberg on April 14, culminating in the drowning of 1517 passengers out of 2224. The main reason was that there were not enough lifeboats on the ship for safety, although the ship is believed to have been the best ever of that time!

Quite interestingly, Robertson had written in his story a lot of similarities about the actual ship Titanic 14 years before it took its maiden journey. The very name of the ship was 'Titan', which was close enough to the actual 'Titanic'! Both are described as the biggest ships of that time and could take a speed of 20 knots. Both were 'unsinkable'! The mishap was taking place in the North Atlantic. Though Robertson is an American writer, he envisaged the story to take place in a British liner. Hitting on an iceberg and the shortage of lifeboats are the other 2 close similarities- one story and the other factual history.

Morgan Robertson Periscope

Once the tragic end of the 'Titanic' came out in the press, Robertson got a lot of publicity. He was more known as a clairvoyant- one who claims to predict the future, which Robertson strongly denied. It was a strange coincidence, according to him.

Robertson, being an expert on maritime trends, might have influenced him while writing the stories.

Inventor of Periscope?

A periscope is an instrument fitted in a submarine that allows the vessel to see targets when submerged if you don't know. Robertson is believed to have claimed to have tried for the patent of a periscope. In any case, he has described a periscope in his novel named 'The Submarine Destroyer' in 1905 and also in other fictional creations.

MASTER SHIPBUILDERS OF INDIA: CRAFTED WORLD-CLASS WARSHIPS FOR ROYAL BRITISH NAVY!

WHAT IS THE HISTORICAL RELATIONSHIP OF NATIONAL ANTHEM OF AMERICA AND INDIA? WHICH IS THE OLDEST SHIP STILL AFLOAT IN THE WORLD? AND WHO BUILT IT?

We all know that as the greatest colonial power on earth, the British once emerged as the 'Empire on which the sun never set' due to their supremacy over the high seas- with their fantastic ships, admirals and sailors. Being an Indian, this I had learned repeatedly right from the the days I started reading as a toddler to this very day. But what I didn't know or learn was that one of the biggest contributions for the British to attain this status rivalling Spain, Portugal or France was colonial India itself!

More than India's rich resources being stolen by them- traders turned as masters- systematically, an Indian shipbuilder at Bombay exclusively built indigenously using Indian craftsmen, skilled workers and raw materials, including Malabar Teak, world-class ships on orders of the British Navy! Not just one or 2 but 363 of them- enabling the British merchant and naval gunships and others trotting the whole globe covering and mastering all the 7 continents in the 17th, 18th and 19th centuries. Such a fleet, which was a product of exclusive Indian brains, skills and technology, contains HMS Minden, HMS Trincomalee and HMS Cornwallis! The name of the great shipbuilder was Jamsetjee Bomanjee, and the family of Wadia Shipbuilders.

More than what you have already read above, it is believed that on board this Indian-made Royal Naval ship HMS Minden, the great American lawyer poet, wrote the US national anthem 'Star- Spangled Banner' while on the coast of the US near Baltimore in 1814! The poet Francis Scott Key was a prisoner in the ship held by the British Navy who also coined and gave America its motto: In God we trust! Again, it was on board HMS Cornwallis, built by Indians in 1842, that the Treaty of Nanking that ceded Hong Kong to the British was signed! Then, the record of the oldest afloat ship goes to HMS Trincomalee, another one.

Hard to believe? Incredible? But be rest assured that this is absolutely true. It is high time that we learn from our own history - our strengths and weaknesses- more than who invaded or colonised and looted us. It is high time that we talk about ourselves and the world rather than waiting for others to do that which they limit to 'extreme poverty or casteism' only for their interests!

HMS Trincomalee is kept at the National Museum of the Royal Navy, England. The figurehead of the ship is modelled on its builder, Jamsetjee Bomanjee.

How I Ran into This

Two months back, I could see a magnificent telefilm video produced by the Indian Navy on themselves. Impressive it was, but I wished that they could add our ancient past too, as the ancient Indian port at Lothal was one of the oldest dry docks in the world, if not the oldest. Subsequently, my interest in digging into the past on the subject hit a gold mine of historical information on our own naval history - of reasonably recent past than ancient ones. That's how I could write this article, which I am sure will raise many eyebrows like I did.

The Background

The Mughals who were ruling India were a bit relieved to see the British East India Company (EIC) in the early 16th century defeating the Portuguese, predominantly because while the latter were Christian fanatics against Islamic fanaticism, the British were not, which went in tune with Mughal's interests in India initially. The Mughals eagerly made concessions to EIC to accommodate them as emperor Jahangir gave them permission to trade within their territory, followed by the commencement of the first British factory at Surat in 1613. Bombay was just a sleepy fishing village then. That status continued till 1662 when Catherine of Braganza of Portugal was given Bombay village as a dowry to wed Charles II of Britain!

At the end of the Napoleonic war against France, after the Battle of Trafalgar in 1815, the British Royal Navy felt the need to replenish their lost or ageing fleet. At that time, there was a shortage of quality oak wood for shipbuilding purposes.

But soon, the British knew about the availability of quality Malabar Teak wood in India, which was even better than oak as it was denser for building ships. Then, bringing the bulky cargo of teak wood to Britain took time, so they focused on the fame of a master shipbuilder at Surat in India, Bomanjee of Wadia Shipbuilders! The British decided to 'outsource' the engineering skill of shipbuilding to an Indian, which was just the tip of the iceberg of events in the naval history of the world to follow.

Portrait of Jamsetjee Bomanjee in British naval archives. A divider is in one hand, while the drawings of HMS Minden are in the other. One can also see the progress of construction of the very ship with 74 guns, which was launched in 1810- also through the window! Interestingly, this portrait is also available in US historical archives for a reason, as explained in the article.

Wadia's Family is the Most Illustrious Shipbuilding Family in the World.

The Wadia Parsi family hails from Surat in Gujarat. The very name 'Wadia' means carpenter/shipbuilder in Gujarati language. Jamset Bomanjee's firm, which was named Surti Ship Builders (later known as Wadia Shipbuilders), secured initial contracts for building ships with EIC from 1736. He himself was the master shipbuilder.

Bombay Dry Docks was built by his brother Lovji Nusserwanjee in 1750 on the British request as EIC headquartered in Bombay from Surat. Incredibly, between 1735 and 1899, 7 generations of Wadias built 363 ships of world-class quality for the British and others, which sailed all over the 7 high seas! The Indian Parsi shipwrights exclusively produced 39 vessels on orders of the British Royal Navy- 16 ships of the line, 13 frigates, 9 sloops and one schooner! Some of them remained the finest creations of its class for decades, which followed! The British, the US and the West have officially chronicled this info, but we Indians are yet to add it to our curriculum for our children, it seems!

Bombay Dock, the oldest in Asia, is functioning even today as the naval Dockyard. The northern part of the erstwhile dockyard is today's Mazagon Dock, India's premier Ship Building Centre.

HMS Minden and Birth of US National Anthem 'Star-Spangled Banner'

This 74-gun frigate had set off for the maiden sail on 8 Feb 1811 from Bombay Dockyard after the customary 'breaking the bottle' ceremony performed by the then British Governor Jonathan Duncan. HMS Minden was the handiwork of Jamshedji for which the order was received from the Royal Navy 10 years earlier. This was the first British Royal Navy ship of the line built out of 'Great' Britain.

Indian-made teak 74 gun ship HMS Minden and actual remains of the US flag are preserved at the National Museum of American History Smithsonian Institute's National Museum of American History.

On 3rd Sept 1814, many Royal Navy ships, including INS Minden, were about to attack US Fort McHenry near the Chesapeake Bay, outside Baltimore, as they were enemies then. On the advice of US President James Madison, 2 of his representatives, Francis Scott Key and John Stuart Skimmer, had set sail on a US boat flying a flag of truce and reached INS Minden. Their aim was peaceful negotiations for surrender with the British. What the British did was not only agree to the discussions but keep the 2 American reps as captives! The night, the royal naval ships bombarded the fort the whole night, to the astonishment of the American captives. In the early morning, expecting complete devastation of the US fort, as they looked out, they could see almost a miracle -the fort was standing loud and clear with a fluttering US flag atop. They believed that God had intervened!

Key was a poet, too. As he saw the US flag with 15 stars and 18 stripes on the fort, he scribbled down a poem while still a captive in the ship, the fragile faded flag remains the holiest icon of American life.

Francis Scott Key original scribbling of the poem

It was recognised as a patriotic song immediately, but it took more than 100 years. On 3rd March 1931, it was declared as the US national anthem.

The last years of HMS Minden were in Hong Kong, where it was used as a hospital before being scrapped in 1861.

HMS Trincomalee and HMS Cornwallis

HMS Trincomalee was launched on 12th October 1987 in Bombay. A 46-gun frigate, it served many occasions for the Royal Navy, including the Crimean War in 1897 and even WWII (1939-1945). It also served as a training ship under the name Foudroyant. To this day, it floats at a British Museum and attracts around 60000 visitors a day!

Guns in HMS Trincomalee

Signing the Treaty of Nanking in HMS Cornwallis

14 gun ship HMS Cornwallis was built in 1813 for the Royal British Navy and served till 1957! The Treaty of Nanking, by which Hong Kong was ceded to Britain, was signed on this Indian-made ship.

The technical prowess and skills of Indians in shipbuilding for the last three centuries are very much recognised in maritime world history. I am neither a professional historian nor a naval architect or expert, but anyone can find these facts in historical chronicles. Am I wrong in suggesting that the subject is to be inducted immediately into the Indian school curriculum, as I find this a 'must' that the whole of India and the world should know?

MICKEY MOUSE HAD TWO FATHERS! REMEMBERING UB IWERKS!

Our grandchildren have now outgrown enjoying cartoon characters like Mickey Mouse. It seems not only Maria has completed her 10 but also Serah, who is 6! Understandable and expected. But my enthusiasm in the subject keeps on going at my 73 plus. I don't know why. The most popular character of all animated cartoons in the world, Mickey Mouse, was created as a rodent with attribution of human rights in 1928- almost 100 years back- by Walt Disney, which is my understanding of the subject. I bet you, too, thought so till this moment. But it was not his lone creation at all! It was a co-creation! His friend and business partner Ub Iwerks animated that character in the initial years while Walt contributed the voice.

Walt Disney himself never hid this matter, at least in the later years of their partnership. In fact, he thought and referred to Ub Iwerks as the greatest animator in the world who animated Mickey's first short, 'Plane Crazy', in 1928. Along with Walt Disney, he co-created, designed, and animated the first version of Mickey Mouse. He was honoured as a 'Disney legend' in 1989. With a peculiar name due to his Dutch origins, his father was a German immigrant to the US who was a barber. And Ub was a dropout of his high school! Walt studied a few more classes but is still a dropout!

Maria and Serah, I am sure that you will read this article someday. A talented person, if she or he can identify it sufficiently early in life and land in the right platform or career, cannot be stopped from becoming a professional in the field. Both of them- Walt Disney and Ub Iwerks- show us their successful professional journeys in spite of all odds, handicaps, and challenges! I could learn this only much later in life, but you can catch up on this simple success story early.

How it all started, ended up and restarted

While Mickey Mouse and Walt Disney are household names in the whole world, Ub Iwerks was never. But in fact, Mickey had 2 dads. It was as teens in 1919 that both met as employees at Pesmen & Rubin Commercial Studio, Kansas City. Soon, both decided to go together on a business of their own. They were both just 21 and landed on a series of failures. In 1922, they opened their first animation studio after acquiring a second-hand movie camera! Started producing advanced films and distributed them in local movie theatres. They also did an animated cartoon series called 'Laugh O Grams'. Soon after, in 1923, they broke up the business as they could not continue successfully.

Along with their own brother Roy, Walt reopened a shop in Hollywood and urged Ub to join them. In 1927, Walt Disney featured his first series of animated films- Oswald the Lucky Rabbit. But soon found that his distributor had the legal rights, and as such, Walt altered the appearance of the rabbit and a new name, "Mortimer Mouse," to make it his own. He also had to change that name at the insistence of his wife Lilian to "Mickey Mouse" soon after. Now, it was the turn of Ub Iwerks, who designed and animated the rodent while Walt gave the sound. That's how, in 1928, both of them co-created and launched the character Mickey Mouse.

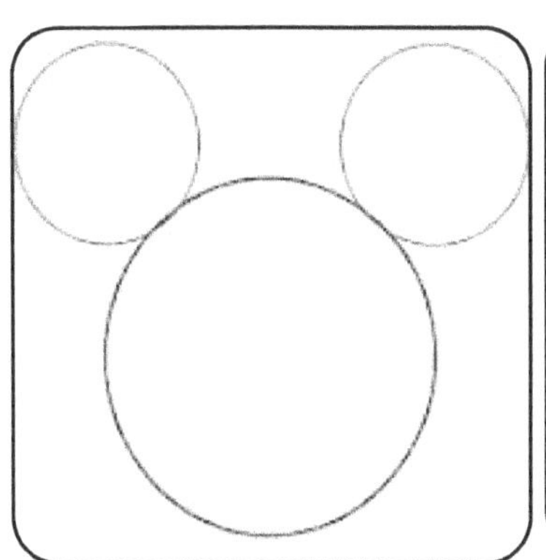

Unfortunately, their business partnership didn't last for long. I could not find the real reason for it, but it seems like their egos clashed. One might have thought that the other would not survive independently! In 1930, they parted to work independently, and later, Ub signed a contract with Pat Powers, Cofounder of Universal Studios, who was a business rival of Walt Studios! In 1936, this firm flopped in business, and eventually, Ub Iwerks rejoined Walt Disney in 1940. Surprisingly, their friendships again flowered, and till 1964, they worked together as if nothing between them had happened. I am sure that they might have realised the strength of the other in those 10 years. Essentially, teamwork brings success to any business.

Later, as the popularity of the most popular cartoon character rose up around the world- with a silhouette of just 3 circles as below- for some reason, only Walt was known about the character Mickey Mouse.

Once Ub Iwerks rejoined Walt Disney in 1940, he had his talents available in special effects to many hit movies like 101 Dalmations, Mary Poppins, The Birds and many more. Ub Iwerks died of a heart attack at the age of 70 in 1971. Ub was nominated 3 times for the Oscar Academy, which he won once. Posthumously, his name was entered into the Hall of Fame award in 2017 by the Visual Effects Society. His granddaughter Leslie Iwerks made a documentary titled 'The Man Behind the Mouse' in 1999.

Three other names of Mickey Mouse

Before I conclude on this subject, I shall also reveal that in at least 3 countries, Mickey Mouse is known by other names. Mickey is known as Musse Pigg in Sweden, Mi Lao Shu in China and Topolino in Italy!

DEDICATION

Mr. N.Govindankutty is no more. He breathed his last on 15th August 2022. He was one of the very best among my close friends and a fine human being. Our friendship lasted over 50 years, but while we were in Qatar, it flowered and blossomed the best. A big loss for me!

Mr Kutty was a senior MEP Project Manager who was a very professional veteran in his field of specialisation in the execution of infrastructure projects. He was himself an acrophile- having no fear of heights- who had successfully contributed his professional service in high-rise structures of Dubai, including Emirates Towers and Burj Khalifa, the tallest in the world!

My tearful bouquet for him. Please rest in peace, 'Kuttysaab', as he was called by me fondly. I am dedicating this article to him today - from the conventional date of every first day of every month- to his Sapindi day to the 16th day of his demise.

MOHAWKS: ACROPHILES OF NEW YORK CITY

The Empire State Building, Rockefeller Centre, The Chrysler Building, George Washington Bridge, United Nations HQ, Time Warner Centre and many others. What is common for all these structures besides that they are all located in Manhattan, NY? Common architects and structural engineers? Construction methodology? Period of construction? None of these.

The common factor is that they are built into record heights by a group of men known as 'Sky Walkers'. But for their nature of having no fear of heights- acrophiles- with their skill in steel construction and riveting, simply it would not have been possible at a time when construction techniques and equipment were not computer-aided and modern as today! And fast they did. The Empire State Building was constructed within one year.

Again, it is not known to the outside world much that most of those 'Sky Walkers' belonged to the Mohawks Indians, a tribe of indigenous people of North America from New York State and Canada! Mohawks were there to construct the World Trade Centre and also to cart away the debris of the same building after it came down on September 9/11. The New York Times once wrote about them: "Lik:e little spiders, they toiled spinning a fabric of steel against the sky.

Mannahatta to Manhattan

Historically, Manhattan Island belonged mainly to the Indian tribe of Lenape before colonisation by Europeans, which was known as 'Mannahatta', meaning 'the place we get bows' in their language. The island was full of Hickory trees considered ideal for bows. Later, it was bought by the Dutch from the Indians, renamed 'New Amsterdam,' and finally emerged as Manhattan. Henry Hudson, an Englishman who worked for the Dutch East India Company, discovered it in 1609. While Manhattan remains the most expensive real estate in the world and showcases some of the most beautifully designed skyscrapers in the modern world, Times Square is the most visited tourist destination in the world- more than 50 million annually! My interest in the skyscrapers of New York never ceases, it seems, and here I am, trying to dig out more on the subject.

The Race for the Tallest Building in the World

The race for the tallest building in the world was not between 2 countries but 2 cities in the same country if you didn't know -Chicago and New York in the late eighties. American Surety

Building in NY in 1895 was the first to be followed by others. However, Chicago won the race later with the opening of Sears Towers in 1974 (now known as Willis Tower). Empire State Building, NY, adorned the title to be the tallest for a long period from 1930 to 1970. Later, it was dwarfed by Petronas Tower in Kuala Lumpur in 1996, Taipie's Taipei in 2004, and the current champion Burj Khalifa in Dubai since 2010.

The first photo above, which was clicked in 1932 at the RFC Building, NY, is iconic. It was on the 69th floor at 850 feet above GL and was publicised as a stunt for the popularity of the building, but it became symbolic with the period of the Great Depression, which was looming large at that time. The same photo is also mistakenly circulated as atop the Empire State Building and Rockefeller Centre! The second photo is what New York looks like from the edge of a skyscraper.

Structural Steel Enters As the Main Building Material in the US

Henry Bessemer of Britain in 1856 remains the father of modern steel making as he could develop a method of producing steel that was quicker and cheaper, followed by William Siemens, who could develop the technology further. However, it was Andrew Carnegie of the US who popularised steel as the main construction material for the skyscrapers of NY and elsewhere. Soon, in the early 20th century, the US surpassed the combined production of Britain and Germany. The huge fire which swept Chicago in 1871 might have surely influenced the designers of a high-rise in NY.

Enter Mohawks

In the 1880s, the Canadian Pacific Railway Company was building a bridge in the Kahnawake Mohawk reservation, and the authorities noticed the special talents of the Mohawk Indians- that they were more or less fearless while working at heights. Soon, they were employed throughout the US, especially in high-rise buildings that were made of steel. From the 1930s to 1970, on special labour contracts, they were employed in Manhattan towers. In those years, we were not as modern as we are today in safety matters- Safety, Health and Environments- SHE or HSE as known in the professional construction field. Many accidents have happened. But those incidents never altered the outlook of the Mohawks towards their dedicated trade!

OSHIYA - THE PROFESSIONAL PUSHERS OF TOKYO METRO!

I had been thinking earnestly that it is in some of the trains and buses in the third world only that passengers are mostly stuffed like sardines in a tiny tin. Though it cannot be compared in the real sense of it, when I saw passengers being pushed professionally inside trains in Tokyo Metro, I got a hiccup! And there are professional pushers named 'Oshiya' employed in Japan. And why, I was curious to find out.

Tokyo caters for 38 million people! And most of them live in far suburbs as the accommodation is expensive and they use public transport systems. While the trains are most modern, fast, and passenger-friendly in queues, the rush hours are simply maddening- with crowds as much as 200% over capacity. I am sure that the authorities must have reached the dead end of facilitating more trains. Instead, they employed passenger pushers to manage the situation.

I understand that Tokyo was not the first city to deploy them, but New York was in the 1920s! Frankfurt, Madrid, and some cities in China use the system to this day! Definitely not on a lighter tone, the youngsters of Kerala state (my home state) who move around the globe looking for new lucrative jobs; this could be a chance if you happen to be in Japan, "Oshiya" of Tokyo!

Most populated city: The need for pushers

Tokyo is the most populated city in the world, followed by Delhi and Shanghai. About 57% of the total population of Japan lives in Tokyo. As the standards of living are higher and costly, most of the common people live in far suburbs. Most of them use public transport systems, mainly trains, to reach their workplaces and shopping areas. The complexity of the Tokyo rail map above reflects the need for such extensive and serpentine railroad systems for metro and other subway trains in that city. At Shin Kunju station in central Tokyo, 1.1 million people board or leave trains daily!

During winter, as the commuters wear warmer and heavier clothes, the spaces get squeezed more practically.

In spite of all the efforts, it seems the authorities might have reached the dead end of introducing more new routes and trains. In peak rush hours, some of the stations are run at 200% over capacity! This was when Japan introduced 'Oshiya' or passenger pushers, taking a clue from New York from 1964 onwards when Japan staged the first Olympics!

Enter the Passenger Pushers

Dressed in full suits and white gloves, the pushers of Tokyo Metro cannot be missed at all during rush hours. These professional pushers are trained for a few weeks before they are deputised for the job. Generally, the Japanese pushers are polite, and passengers cooperate with them when being pushed in. They might have learned a lesson or 2 from New York rail pushers who were hated by commuters for being rude, and they were known as 'sardine packers'! At times, college students are also employed to allow them to earn extra money! Interestingly, the train passengers are almost silent despite being pushed in! At Lost & Found, piles of shoes, handbags, tie pins, or books are reported to be exhibited at every station soon after rush hours. Not only the passengers but these pushers also contribute their efforts in this matter.

On average, they are paid an annual salary of $44995 (Rs. 40 lakhs!) for this weird job.

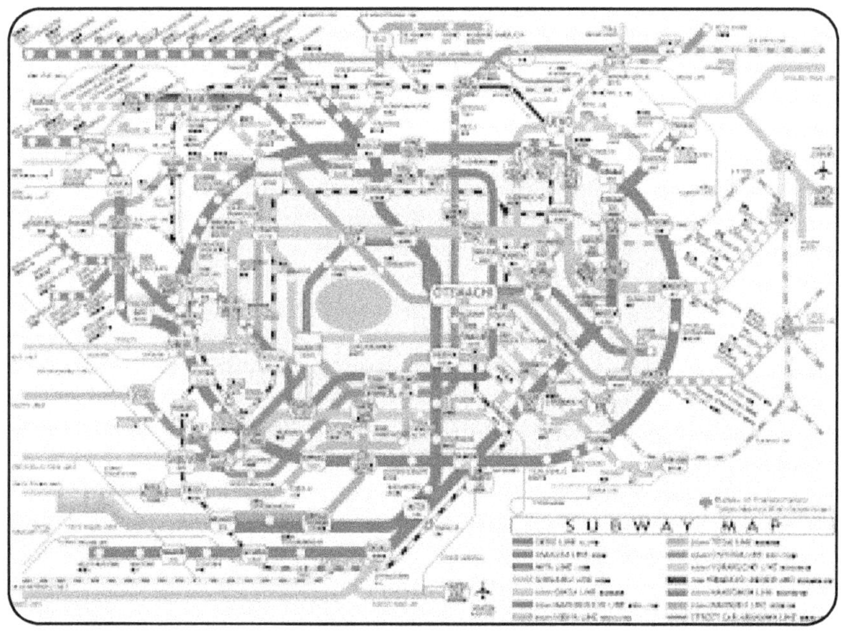

Pushers of China, Spain, Germany

In China, at least 3 metros, Shanghai, Chongqing, and Guangzhou, have been using pushers at peak rush hours since 2008. At Madrid Metro, pushers are known as 'empujadores' and have been employed since 2017. At Frankfurt Metro, especially while the famous trade fair takes place there, they have sought the help of pushers since 2015.

PEPSI: HOW THEY OWNED THE SIXTH-LARGEST NAVAL FLEET IN THE WORLD!

Undoubtedly, the names Coke and Pepsi remain the 2 most popular soft drink brands in the world from their inception in 1886 and 1893, respectively.

Pepsi, started by a small-town pharmacist named Caleb D Bradham, was selling his product initially under the name 'Brad's Drink'. He bought the name 'Pep Kola' from a local competitor in North Carolina, US and changed the name to Pepsi Cola. PepsiCo had to go through many ups, downs and bottleneck situations and became bankrupt at least once. Had to change ownerships but appreciatively continued to grow along with Coke- rivals to this day! I am not here to tell you more about them or their rivalry, which is well-known to all of us.

Here I am for a narration of how PepsiCo came to own a Soviet Naval Fleet! How Pepsi Navy all of a sudden became the sixth-largest in the world in 1989. This is not fiction. This is real history. Before the fall of the Soviet Union (USSR), they traded 20 warships with the American Beverage Company PepsiCo! The thirst for Pepsi Cola among the Russians compelled them to do that once.

1959 American National Exhibition in Moscow

Iron Curtain period. In the US, it was the tenure of President Dwight D Eisenhower and Richard Nixon as Vice President. That was also when Nikita Khrushchev, as Premier of the USSR, honestly believed that life under Communist rule was better than in the Capitalist US and vice versa. Moreover, the propaganda of the USSR was that their economic system was far superior to that of the US and may overtake them soon! I remember reading free periodicals issued by USIS (United States Information Service) and 'Soviet Land' of USSR, both claiming themselves to be the best in the world! Indian Prime Minister Nehru and their daughter Indira Gandhi were also mesmerised by the Soviet claims who very often conducted tours in the USSR and tried to implement 'Socialism' in India as well until when India took a U-turn in the late 90s and headed for Capitalism, though not fully yet!

President Eisenhower took a chance and decided to participate in 1959 and showcase their products in Moscow. Thus, many US companies in the Govt and Private sectors, like Kodak, General Electric, McDonald's, Pizza Hut, Baskin Robbins, etc, decided to participate. Pepsi also joined the delegation represented by CEO Donald Kendal, while Coca-Cola decided not to (see the photo below).

At the exhibition hall, on the first day of the inaugural function, when Khrushchev visited the stall of Pepsi, he was offered Pepsi to taste by CEO Donald Kendall in the presence of Nixon. Khrushchev fell for the drink immediately! He ordered the concerned to negotiate with the Pepsi team and settle the order to make Pepsi available in the country. The exhibition was visited by 2.7 million Soviets.

The Problem of Currency Surfaces

Soviet's own currency, the Rouble, had no value outside the country, and Americans expressed their inability to execute the order. The problem was finally resolved by the USSR amicably. Americans will have state-owned vodka named Stolichnaya against payment to Pepsi! A sort of barter system. Thus, the US and USSR had a successful deal, which could be for the first time during the Iron Curtain period. Kendall eventually negotiated a landmark deal to mass-produce Pepsi in the USSR.

One of the catchy advertisements of Pepsi those days was: 'Be sociable, Have a Pepsi". When the photo of Khrushchev sipping Pepsi came out in newspapers around the world, the wording of the advertisement was changed to: 'Khrushchev learns to be Sociable'! The Westerners are very good at wry humour to this day, I admit.

Khrushchev learns to be 'sociable'!

Pepsi gets a Soviet Naval Fleet

Pepsi and the Soviets didn't have any problems, and business flourished till 1980. That was the year the USSR invaded Afghanistan. The American people, for political reasons, responded by boycotting products of the USSR, including Stolichnaya vodka! Pepsi had a real problem then.

The Soviets finally resolved the matter in 1989, offering a veritable navy owned by them. Pepsi agreed to the offer, which included 17 submarines, a cruiser, a frigate and a destroyer. In the same year, tanks rolled into Tiananmen Square, and the notorious Berlin Wall fell in Germany- events which shook the Communist world just before the downfall of Communism in the USSR itself in 1991.

Tail Piece

1. PepsiCo never had a navy of their own in reality since they didn't take possession of the fleet. As the vessels were in a very old and unseaworthy condition, PepsiCo, as the fleet came to them to be owned, immediately turned them over to a Norwegian Shipyard to be scrapped to raise the money the Soviets owed to them!

2. In 2004, Kendall received the Order of Friendship from Russian President Putin!

3. Russia remained Pepsi's second-largest international market after Mexico until April 2022. Following Russia's invasion of Ukraine, PepsiCo has suspended their operations in Russia.

SOKUSHINBUTSU: SELF-MUMMIFICATION WHILE ALIVE

We all know that 'mummification' is the process of preserving a dead body as 'mummy'. We also know it was a practice in Egypt, probably around 2500 BC. Who hasn't heard of Tutankhamun? That practice is well-known in Egypt, and a few other countries also practised earlier and later than Egypt, like Chile, China and Korea.

They all believed in the afterlife after death. They also believed that the soul could be repossessed after death if only a form (body) existed. Adapting to special techniques, all the moisture in the dead body is removed to a dried state, and thousands of years back, there were clear steps to do the mummification process. The word 'mummy' is based on the Latin 'Mumia', derived from Arabic 'Mumiya', which means embalmed corpse.

But have you heard of self-mummification? That is, one indulges in the process of mummification while being alive. Yes, this was there in Japan among certain sects of Buddhist monks until the 19th century when the Japanese government thankfully banned it by law. Personally, I don't have reverence for such acts, which are nothing more than suicidal and meaningless. But since it is part of what man has done to attain 'nirvana' is to be known.

Sokushinbutsu

In Japanese, it is the process of self-mummification. There are 3 segments in the school of Buddhism: Hinayana, Mahayana, and Vajrayana, which hail from India. Among Vajrayana under the sect of Shingon founded by Kukai in the 7th century, this process was once practised. Temples in villages surrounding Mount Yudono in Japan have quite a number of such self-mummified monks.

Process of self-mummification.

It takes 8-10 years for a monk to attain this. It starts with a strict diet of just pine needles, seeds, nuts and raisins. During 3 years of this diet, the monk loses all the body fat. Then, for the next 3 years, they eat only particular tree bark and selective roots. After 6 years or so, they start drinking tea made of the sap of a tree named Urushi, which is poisonous! It also kills the maggots or insects that would cause decay of the body once dead.

In the last leg of the process, the monk locks himself in a stone tomb and sits in a lotus position. The tomb will have a tube connecting to outside air so that he can breathe. It will also have a bell, which the monks will ring once a day to announce to others that he is alive. Once the ringing stops, it is known to others that he is dead.

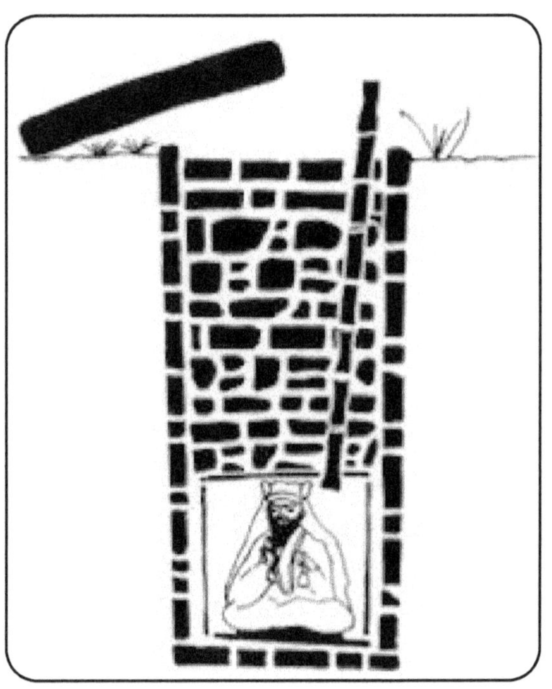

Mummy of Lin Quan

The story of the mummy of Lin Quan is interesting and baffling. During the Song dynasty (960-1297) of China, a Buddhist monk made himself a mummy. He was a popular man among the people, helpful and just. As such, his body remains were enclosed inside a golden statue of Buddha, hardly known to the outside world. His remains were worshipped for nearly 1000 years. During the cultural revolution of Mao in China, this statue was hidden and buried. It was there till 1995 when the local villagers found it missing until it surfaced in Hong Kong!

Later, it was purchased by a few art lovers and collectors and landed in the Hungarian Museum in 2015, reportedly purchased by an Amsterdam-based architect and collector. It was also displayed in other museums in Europe. The villagers of China wanted the monk badly and booked a case against the possessor in a Dutch court. Chinese Govt backed up its people. Meanwhile, the photo of the Buddha taken by the CT scan went viral among art lovers around the world. A legal battle took place, and finally, the Dutch court dismissed the case in 2018, finding that the villagers have no such right to reclaim! Now, to the best of my knowledge, the Buddha is in possession of a Chinese businessman, and further whereabouts are not known since the Chinese government might have placed an embargo on further news.

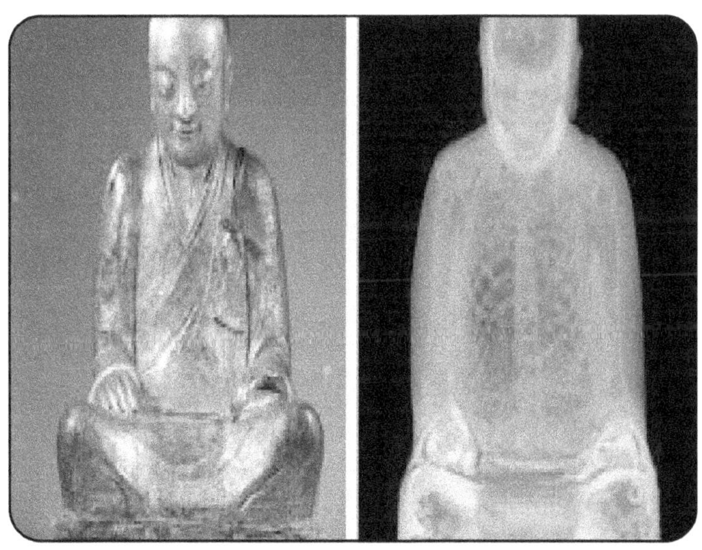

In India, too, at least a single case of self-made mummy is there. It is located in Himachal Pradesh, a place on the borders of Tibet. Even if it is only one, I think we should let the world know it, especially for those foreign Buddhists who throng India as the birthplace of Gautama Buddha and even for Indian nationals and other tourists to know our diversity in culture!

TENNO HEIKA BANZAI

On October 25, 1944, the Japanese military employed Kamikaze bombers for the first time in WW2. Who's a Kamikaze bomber? He is the specially trained pilot who would crash his specially made plane directly into Allied ships. Simply put, a Kamikaze attack is a suicidal bombing tactic to destroy enemy ships.

Mohotoru Okamura, who commanded a Kamikaze Squadron, sincerely believed that these daredevil acts would make the tide of war in favour of Japan as he ordered the first Kamikaze pilot to be at the battle of Leyte Gulf in the Pacific Ocean near the Philippines!

In various attacks after that, more than 3000 Japanese Kamikaze pilots perished, while causalities among the US, Australian and British forces might have touched 7000. Nevertheless, this did not change the tide of war. Japan had to surrender unconditionally on August 16 1945!

"Tenno Heika Banzai" literally means "Ten Thousand Years" in Japanese. This they used to express joy or long life. It was also used by the Japanese military personnel while storming in the battle, meaning "Long Live The Emperor". The Kamikaze pilot used to shout exactly these words before he hit the ship of Allied Forces, killing himself!

KAMIKAZE STRIKES: JAPAN'S LAST BID FOR VICTORY!

The year 1944: Birth Of Kamikaze.

By the year 1944, it was clearer that the tide of World War was clearly favouring the Allied forces. Japan, one of the trailing Axis Forces, was facing defeat one after another, whether on land, sea or air. It was in this context that Takijiro Onishi, Admiral of the Imperial Japanese Navy, who founded Kamikaze, convinced his superiors to have a squadron of suicide bombers attack and destroy enemy ships to change the tide of war. At least they would be able to negotiate better terms for surrender, Japan thought. But Takijiro had to commit ritual suicide following the unconditional surrender of Japan!

Kamikaze means 'divine wind'. It was the name of a typhoon that originally destroyed invading Mongol ships in the 13th century, saving Japan.

Kamikaze Planes

The planes used were light bombers loaded with bombs-250 kg on the nose and extra gasoline tanks. Kamikaze planes were launched with their wheels dropped at take-off. This reduces the weight, increases the range and possibly limits the ability of the pilot to return. These single-seated planes- mostly like Yokosuka MX 7 Okha were used.

Kaiten: Torpedoes containing human beings!

Kaitens were an underwater equivalent of Kamikaze. These were launched from submarines for direct combat on identified ships. The kitchen was small enough for the pilot to squeeze through and enter the body of the torpedo! The pilot verifies the position of the target- a ship normally- by a fitted periscope and then surges for the final assault. The first Kaiten assault claimed USS Mississinewa, which was on anchor when hit. 63 US sailors perished.

Kamikaze pilots' training

Kamikaze pilots were given special training for their special mission. They performed a special ceremony of drinking Sake (Rice wine) and eating rice before they took off on their mission. They were also honoured by giving medals and a Katana sword (traditional curved sword used by Samurai) during these ceremonies.

By 1945, more than 500 Kamikaze planes had taken part in these suicide missions, it is estimated! And 3800 Kamikaze pilots had died. Many were new recruits from the finest universities in Japan! Although Kamikaze pilots never threatened to change the course of war led by the Allied forces, Kamikaze offensives were a concern for the Allies.

A number of books and movies have been produced based on the actual experiences of Kamikaze post-war.

THE DAY RUSSIA COMPLETELY RAN OUT OF VODKA

Vodka is synonymous with Russia, like Alfred Hitchcock with thriller movies. Vodka is more of a symbol of Russia to rival its own brown bears, caviars and Matryoshka! Sure, vodka is native of Russia, with the highest consumption rate among the people for the last many centuries, currently with 17 shots per person per month! Poland and Ukraine are close enough to them in this matter. So, the whole of the vodka belt containing Eastern Europe and Nordic countries.

The word vodka comes from the translation of water in Russian, "Voda." Experts suggest that its use has become so common among the people in Russia because it is a quick remedy for the cold they have to face! Vodka is everywhere in Russia, in politics, folk songs, movies, literature, and jokes, which have become inseparable from people's social lives.

Having narrated about the importance of vodka in the life of Russia and Russians, there was a time when they ran out of vodka for a day and had to face disrupted supply for many following days! That was on May 9, 1945, the day Germany surrendered to the Allied Forces as officially announced by Russia on the radio. The news broke out on that day by 1.10 am, but the Soviet citizens went outside in the middle of the night in their pyjamas, embraced each other and wept with joy. Before Stalin could officially announce the German surrender, the country had run out of vodka.

Russia has not changed

In 2017, much later, after the Soviet Union had disintegrated into so many countries, including Russia, Geetha and I were in Moscow along with a few other Indians on tour. As we visited a good restaurant for a buffet dinner, there was a free offer from the owner that either a can of beer or a shot of locally brewed vodka was free. As expected, hardly a few fellow Indians had it, but those who had gone for international brands of beer. But I went for the vodka since I thought it was a good chance to taste the local brew of Moscow. Sure, as practised, I wanted soda or water to dilute it, but the bartender asked me to take it as it was in sips. It was a good decision, and I ordered the second shot. Geetha joked that it was a clever ploy of the owner to extract money. But when we wanted to settle the bill, I was not charged for the vodka in spite of being asked to bill the extra shot! The waiter smilingly told me that it was in the house! Their love for vodka has not changed a bit whether the Govt has become capitalist or Communist or dictatorship.

Origin of Vodka

Poles claim that they had been making vodka since the 8th century, distilling grain and potato spirits. However, Russia started it much later in the 14th century. It is believed that an orthodox monk of Greek origin named Isidore had pioneered it in 1430, distilling from Chudov monastery in Moscow distilling products of wheat and hence known as 'bread wine.'

Chudov Monastery

In 1472, Tsar Ivan II institutionalised the first state autonomy of vodka in the country. All in Russia had to purchase the state-produced vodka except the nobles of the society, who were permitted to brew. Thus, home-brewed vodka is infused with herbs, berries, and fruits. Peter the Great invented the 'penalty shot'- a shot of vodka - but in a goblet of 1.5 litres- to be gulped by those who came late to his parties. The first prohibition was also imposed during the Tsarist reign. Tsar Nicholas did that in

1914. I don't know whether it had any impact on the Bolshevik revolution, which followed soon.

When the Communist revolution came in 1917, it did not curb the people's interest in vodka either since it was a good way of collecting revenue. In fact, the production, distribution, and sales of vodka became more professional. During the Second World War, the Soviet soldiers were supplied with 100 grams of vodka each day.

Smirnoff Vodka is not a Russian Brand

Smirnoff, who fled Russia during the revolution period, established his brand of vodka in the USA, Canada, and many other western countries. Made from grains of wheat, corn, and potatoes, this brand is the largest-selling brand in the world, and it is found in 130 countries where vodka is used! The second most-sold vodka brand is Absolut, a Swedish product! Besides the quality of these products, western techniques of advertising and sales might have helped establish these brands in the world in popularity, I presume.

THE FIRST COMPUTER PROGRAMMER IN THE WORLD

Bill Gates to Steve Jobs, Linus Torvalds to Mark Zuckerberg, Guido Van Rossum to Bjarne Stroustrup. not forgetting the great Tim Berners-Lee, creator of the World Wide Web. all could be some of the most well-known computer programmers of the world's successful professionals in the field. But who the first computer programmer was could be a wild guess for many.

It is Ada Lovelace. Her name could be very unfamiliar among many of us. But we all have heard about her well-known father -the poet Lord Byron! She is considered to be the only legitimate daughter he had, and her mother was Anne Isabella Milbanke, an excellent Mathematician of her time! Ada was a product of wedlock, which didn't last long, and it was a product of romantic poetry and intricate maths and science.

Though Lord Byron's creations were very popular, his private life was not. Finally, he had to leave Britain for good and spend years in some of the Mediterranean countries. Here, I am to write about how Byron's daughter became a renowned computer programmer of her time. At a time when computer programming vigorously continues to expand in artificial intelligence and machine learning (AI and ML), the internet of things (IoT), quantum computing, and beyond, her contribution becomes more relevant.

How Ada Byron becomes Ada Lovelace

Her original name was Ada Augusta Byron. Lord Byron's other children, other than Ada, were all half-siblings. Her mother was Anne Isabella Milbanke - more popular as Lady Byron- an excellent and intelligent Mathematician herself. She was also an active Educational Reformer and Abolitionist who wanted to abolish slavery in the world. Interestingly, poet Byron used to call her by her nickname - 'Princess of Parallelograms'! A person with a Maths background may understand the fun in properties of this shape, while others have to excuse me! Lord Byron had an immoral life, it seems, and their relationship as husband and wife broke without long.

Lord Byron had to leave Britain and spent the rest of his life in Mediterranean countries. Lord Byron left when Ada was just one month old. He died in Greece when Ada was 8. Ada was married to William King in 1835, who later was made Earl of Lovelace, thus becoming Countess Lovelace.

Ada's schooling and how she became a computer enthusiast!

Ada did not have a formal way of schooling or University studies; instead, she was tutored by eminent teachers. Like her mother, Ada was taught Maths and Science at a young age. As she grew up, she was very much exposed to the elite class of Victorian London, like Michael Faraday, Charles Dickens and Mary Somerville. At that time, the Lucasian professorship of Maths at the University of Cambridge was held by a scientist engineer named Charles Cabbage. It could be interesting to note that Sir Isaac Newton was in that position earlier, as well as Stephen Hawking in later years. Ada was fascinated by the computing machine derived by Charles Babbage, which was known as "The Analytical Engine," the first-ever automatic digital computer.

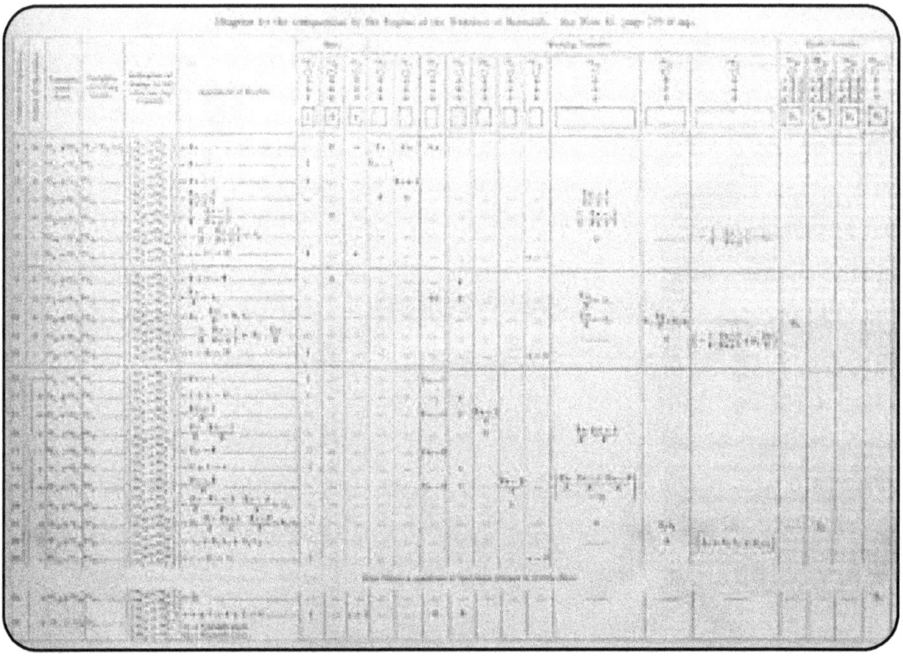

The analytical engine and calculation of Bernoulli numbers

In 1843, she published a translation from the French of an article on the Analytical Engine by an Italian engineer, Luigi Menabrea, to which Ada added extensive notes of her own. Ada's thoughts about using the machine were very familiar to present-day programmers. Her paper on the machine and the program she wrote are regarded as extraordinary accomplishments. Only very few recognised her talents at her time, yet perfectly understandable 2 centuries later! From a modern perspective, her work was a visionary.

No wonder in 1979, the US Dept of Defence created its own computer language, which was named 'ADA' to honour her contributions.

Ada Dies at a Young Age

At the age of only 36, she died of Uterine Cancer in 1852. In spite of this, her mother never gave her a chance to talk about her father, Lord Byron; she was interested in her father as she grew older. As per her wish, her body was buried next to her father in Greece!

THE MOST EXPENSIVE BOOK EVER SOLD AND THE VITRUVIAN MAN

He never had a real educational background or attended any renowned institution of his time. His education was limited to being taught to read and write and do elementary Mathematics, though he was interested in dissecting human bodies to study human Anatomy, which is reflected in the paintings he made later! He was a successful engineer who conceptualised a helicopter in the late 14th century. He was an innovator, scientist, sculptor, architect, anatomist, musician, writer and painter- one of the very best the world has created in each category.

He left about 6000 pages of journal in his own hand behind him. And mysteriously, it was in reverse. This meant that anyone could read them only by holding to a mirror! One such 72-page notebook, which was written between 1506 and 1510, furnished a wealth of sketches and diagrams mostly related to the earth, Moon and the sun. In 1994, a wealthy book collector bought it for $ 30.8 million, which happens to be the most expensive book ever sold! The buyer was Bill Gates, Founder of Microsoft, while the author was Leonardo da Vinci! Vinci is the name of his village since he could not use his family name as he was illegitimate.

For the common man, 2 of his paintings -Mona Lisa and The Last Supper- are the most famous. But here I would like to share about his iconic painting known as 'Vitruvian Man'. The first 2 paintings show Leonardo's artistic talents, while

the latter exhibits his scientific knowledge, which was much ahead of his time.

Marcus Vitruvius

He was a Roman military, civil engineer and architect who served Julius Caesar around 57 BC. He was known for writing a treatise, 'De Architectra', which was a combination of history with engineering talents along with Science, Mathematics, Medicine, Metrology and even Philosophy! He sums up 3 qualities of any building- beauty, stability and utility! It may sound simple and logical today, but he did that some 2000 years ago! The book had 10 chapters. In chapter I of book III, Vitruvius described the proportions of the human body based on which Leonardo da Vinci created the 'Vitruvian Man'! The oldest copy available dates to the 8th century. The drawing illustrates a nude man in 2 superimposed positions inscribed in squire as well as a circle.

How and Why was 'Vitruvian Man ' Created by Leonardo?

Leonardo is regarded as a Renaissance painter who was very keen on human Anatomy all along. The facts on human body proportions of a man introduced by Marcus Vitruvius were attracted by him in symmetry and balance, bridging the gap between art and Mathematics. In 1490, Leonardo made a sketch 24.5*34.3 centimetres in size with pen and ink, along with surrounding notes.

Leonardo chose to depict the man with 4 legs and 4 arms, allowing him to strike 16 poses simultaneously! It is kept at Galleria dell 'Accademia' in Venice, which I never knew about when I visited the place about 10 years back. It has been there since 1872, and I was thinking for some reason that all da Vinci creations are kept at the Louvre in Paris. It was once exhibited at the Louvre in 2009 to mark the 500th anniversary of Leonardo's Death. Nobody knows the monetary value, but it is insured for a billion Euros.

To sum up, the 'Vitruvian Man' is the sketch of the body of a perfect man! Da Vinci has also noted down some of his scientific observations. From the roots of the hair to the bottom of the chin, it is 1/10 th of a man's height. The beginning of the genitals marks the middle of the man. A person's arm span is equal to his height, etc. Da Vinci inspired many other Renaissance painters, such as Raphael.

IQ rating of Leonardo

His IQ rating is estimated to be 180-220, which means he is one of the best anyone has in this universe. That could be the reason that he was one of the most diversely talented people to have ever lived on this planet.

THE ONLY CITY WHICH IS NAMED AFTER AN AUTOMOBILE BRAND

The practice of naming cars after towns and cities by automobile manufacturers worldwide has been common for the last many decades. Austin Westminster, Kia Rio, Chevrolet Tahoe, Ferrari California, and Bentley Mulsanne are just a few examples I took randomly from the long list of such cars. But do you know that in a country a major city is named after a brand of automobile and not the other way around?

Definitely, it is not Detroit (USA). However, it has been known as 'motor city' as a sobriquet for over the last 100 years due to the presence of huge manufacturing facilities of General Motors, Ford or Chrysler. It is not Wolfsburg in Germany, where it is the hub of VW and a few others, or Stuttgart, where 2 automobile museums named Mercedes-Benz Museum and Porche Museum exist, known as the cradle of automobiles. It is neither Modena in Italy where Ferrari or Maserati is built.

Toyota City in Japan. That's it. Previously known as Koroma till 1959, the name was changed to Toyota City to reflect the major employer of the town- Toyota Motor Corporation. It is an industrial city East of Nagoya in Aichi Prefecture in central Japan where more than 426000 people live with all modern amenities. Understandably, Toyota City is a sister city of Derby (UK), where Toyota has a manufacturing unit, and also of Detroit (USA)

Two landmarks at Toyota City: stadium and the bridge

Why Toyota was Honoured by Toyota City

Toyota, as we all know, is the most popular brand of car in the world, with a major market share in as many as 44 countries. In Yemen, it jumps to 93%! Toyota retained its spot as the number one global maker even in 2021. Records show that 4 out of 5 most popular cars ever sold in the world are Toyotas. The first position goes to the Toyota Hilux, then the Toyota Corolla and the third is the Toyota Landcruiser, which is an SUV. This is an incredible automobile because I myself had the chance to use 5 models in 21 years while in Qatar. The fourth position goes to the Skoda Octavia, but again, the fifth goes to the Toyota RAV.

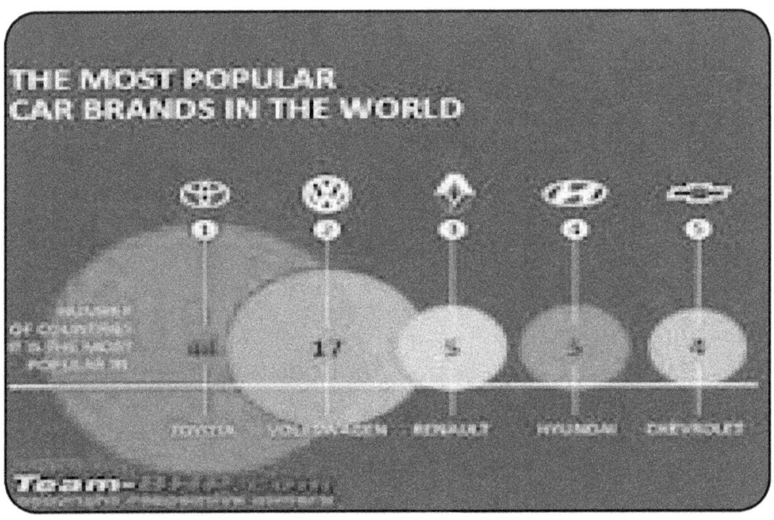

The history of car making in Japan dates back to 1912-26. After WWI, a few corporations, like Toyota and Nissan, started producing trucks. After WWII, after the defeat of Japan by the Allied forces, Japan was barred from producing cars till 1950! However, in 1959, Japan started exporting cars to the US, and Toyota became the first brand to do so! In 2008, Toyota became the largest manufacturer of automobiles, surpassing General Motors in the USA.

Aichi is one of the 47 prefectures- administrative divisions- of Japan. Located in the East of Kyoto in central Japan, Aichi prefecture is considered to be the capital of Japanese Industrialisation manufacturing, from pottery to textiles to cars and aeroplanes. Obviously, most of Toyota's 16 factories are located in this city! Two landmarks of Toyota City which stand out are its stadium and the bridge, which were designed by Japanese architect Kisho Kurokawa. With a unique retractable roof and seating capacity of 45000, the stadium hosted the FIFA World Cup of Japan in 2012. The city also caters to the public with a lot of museums.

History of Car Making by Toyota in Japan

Sakichi Toyoda, founder of Toyota, started with a textile business in 1924. He developed Toyoda Model G Automatic Loom and started producing them industrially by forming a company called Toyoda Automatic Loom Works Ltd. However, as soon as it was decided to enter the automobile market, this company happened to be the forerunner of Toyota Industries Corporation. Toyota was a family business, and even now, it continues to have the same status with Akio Toyoda as CEO.

How the Name of Toyoda Became Toyota

This could be an interesting story unknown to many. Sure, the family name was 'Toyoda', which means "fertile rice patty' in Japanese, while 'Toyota' has no specific meaning. Then why was the name changed?

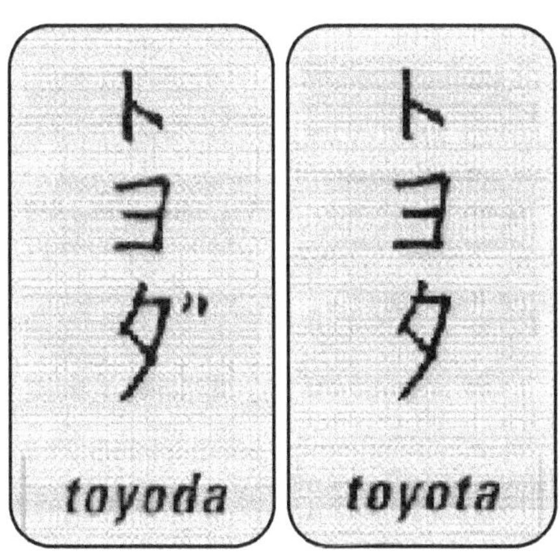

It takes 10 strokes to write 'Toyoda' in Japanese, while it takes only 8 strokes to write 'Toyota'. Eight is considered a lucky and auspicious number in Japan. Hence, the owners went for the Toyota.

Three overlapping eclipses

The motto behind the logo is also interesting to know. The column-like eclipse perched on the top represents the unification of the hearts of Toyota customers and Toyota products. The final eclipse, the one that surrounds the other 2, represents Toyota's drive for technical inventions and futuristic opportunities!

THE TRAFFIC JAM AT BRANDENBURG GATE!

The worst traffic jam that ever happened in the world was in China in August 2010 on the Beijing-Tibet Expressway. It lasted for an incredible 12 days! The drivers could move only 1 km per day! One bottle of water, which cost only 1 Yuan, was sold on this highway for 15 during that time. So also noodles and cigarettes. There are similar incidents elsewhere in the world. In February 2011, in Chicago, Illinois, and in Bethel, New York, in 1969. Each traffic jam- small or big- anywhere in the world is a harrowing experience for those who have experienced it.

But here I am writing about a traffic jam- a gateway to a new world- which happened in Berlin, Germany, in April 1990. Berlin Wall was brought down piece by piece by jubilant crowds of East Germany on 9 November 1989. It was estimated to be 18 million cars on the roads on 12 April 1990- it was the Easter holidays- during the unification process full of Germans eager to reconnect with friends and family members with a fallen Berlin Wall, which many thought to remain forever, I included. Many East Germans thought that the borders that were now open could be closed anytime later! Instead, it turned out to be a peaceful revolution. It eventually stopped the Iron Curtain and started the process of the demise of Communism in the world! Neither a shot was fired, nor anyone died.

The aftermath of the defeat of Germany in WW II

After the utter defeat of Germany and Axis forces- unconditional surrender- in WWII, the jubilant Allied forces agreed by a common decision to divide Germany into 4 zones occupied, namely Britain, USA, USSR and France. The capital, Berlin, too, was so divided. Such a decision was made at a high-level meeting at Yalta. You may note that Yalta is in Livadiya, Crimea, which was a part of Ukraine but forcibly incorporated by Russia as the Republic of Crimea. The palace where the meeting took place on February 4-11,1945, was the former summer retreat of the last Russian Tsar Nicholas and their family.

The zones taken by Britain, the USA and France became West Germany (Federal Republic of Germany), practising Capitalism and a free market economy, while the USSR zone became East Germany (German Democratic Republic), practising Communism. Both came into existence in 1949.

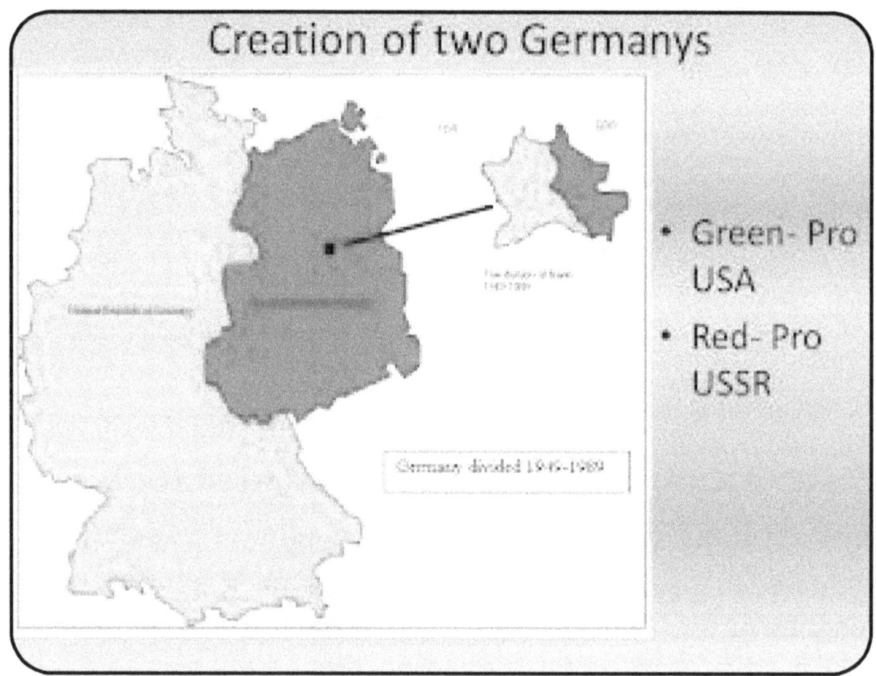

Brandenburg Gate

Brandenburg Gate, which is Berlin's most popular landmark to date, is a monument gateway which reminds us of the Acropolis, Greece. This gate was built by King Fredrich William II in 1788-1791. The Quadriga on the top of it depicts a two-wheeled chariot pulled by four horses side by side to symbolise peace entering the city when erected. In 1806, Napoleon took home this chariot, which was brought back 8 years later. During the division of Germany, this gate could be visited neither by West Germans nor by those from the East, albeit it is situated in the USSR sector. The gate symbolised symbol of Germán division, but later, it symbolised German unification!

Why and how was the Berlin Wall erected and brought down?

Right from the start, life in East Germany was less attractive compared to that in the West. Salaries were much less, and so was freedom. As such, a lot of Easterners moved to West Germany for work in spite of restrictions on visas. From 1949 to 1961, more than 2.7 million East Germans, especially blue-collar workers and professionals, moved to the West. While the GDR proclaimed through propaganda that life in the West was only an illusion, the fact was something different. I knew this in person since one of my elderly neighbours, who was very friendly towards my brother and me in 1965 or so, was a member of some sort of club linked to the GDR and USSR! He used to tell me about the USSR and GDR those days, but my brother used to hear VOA (Voice of America) broadcasts regularly and get literature from USIS (United States Information Service) on a regular basis. He used to tell me what our neighbour told us was false!

However, as history unfolded for me, on the night of 13 August 1961, the East German authorities stopped the movement by erecting a barbed wire fence through the heart of Berlin, which later changed to concrete structures for fortifications. Plus, the entire border of East Germany was laid with 1 million land mines and 3000 attack dogs, along with 302 watch towers with ready-to-shoot at-sight orders! The official explanation of East Germany was that this wall would prevent fascists of West Germany from infiltrating the East. But actually, the only aim was to stop or control the defections of East Germans to the West, which they were ashamed to admit.

On 12 June 1987, in a speech at the Brandenburg Gate, US President Ronald Reagan challenged Mikhail Gorbachev, leader of the USSR, to tear down the wall. Two years later, on November 9, 1989, the jubilant East Germans actually tore down the wall piece by piece, as you can see in the photos above. On October 3, 1990, East and West Germany were unified to be known as Germany officially! Communism was a good idea but proved to be Utopian! Long live freedom, equality and fraternity.

"THERE ARE SUCH THINGS AS FALSE TRUTHS AND HONEST LIES!"

I always wanted to write about Romani people, but for no specific reason, I left it like that. I was reading the other day about Hitler's long list of people whom he hated and persecuted for his own reasons. We know all about the Jews and what he did to them. But others who were featured in his notorious list were Romani, Poles, Afro-Germans, those who practised Jehovah's Witnesses, people with disabilities and homosexuals! Most of them sincerely believed that they were culturally inferior or unwilling to accept a Nazi takeover of the helm of affairs in Germany! It is estimated that Hitler killed 2 million Romani people.

Here, I shall focus on Romani people. Many of you might not have understood who they were! For an easier understanding, I shall use a word which is used widely to this day for them, though they consider it as derogatory-gypsies! Yes, Romani is a Gypsy. Romani people are descendants of many groups who left India for good, belonging to Gujjars, Chauhan, Sansi and a few others from Punjab and the north Indian region in the 10th century! Yes, they are originally Indians. Thereafter, they lived in Europe, although basically a nomad, having no permanent house and always on the move. Romani language is close to Sanskrit and Hindi.

They had a humiliating life all along in Europe, but many famous writers, singers, artists, footballers, and politicians are from this community, including Charlie Chaplin, Pablo Picasso and

Elvis Presley! For the title of this article, I have used a Romani proverb.

Origin of Romani people

Romani people originated in India, for sure. They are believed to have entered Eastern Europe in the 10th century from the Punjab region of India as nomads. The Europeans mistakenly believed that they were from Egypt, and the name Gyspy got stuck to them. The original gypsies were not well educated, and no historians were among them. It is as late as the 18th century that the origin was correctly identified by the Europeans.

Many of Romani people traditionally worked as craftsmen, blacksmiths, cobblers, tool makers and horse dealers. But a lot of famous musicians, writers, politicians, actors, footballers, and even evangelists are there! They speak a language close to Sanskrit and Hindi, along with Punjabi. Their language is largely unwritten.

The Romani people could have been Hindus, but now they are mostly Christians- Catholics or Orthodox. There are some Muslims also among them.

Thousand Years of Discrimination Still On

Most of the Romani people, whether in Europe or elsewhere, live in very poor socio-economic conditions. Very unfortunate situation even now. They face discrimination and segregation in almost all the countries in which they live!

In many countries, they have passed laws to suppress the culture of Romani and to keep them out of the mainstream. In a survey conducted, it was found that more than half of the Europeans don't want gypsies as neighbours! It is also a fact that the Romani people have 10 years less in life expectancy compared to other 'white' Europeans! Romani people were enslaved in Hungry and Rumania in the 15th century. Hitler thought that the Romans had an inferior culture and placed them on par with the Jews in the Holocaust! Most of them were sent to the infamous Auschwitz camp! Their misery is still in the dark since there is hardly any written history of their sufferings, unlike Jews! Even the champion of democracy, the

US, is not fair to them in treatment, I understand. But I don't think that Indians are eligible to complain since we are good at ill-treating even our own folks even now in spite of the laws being in place!

Romani Ancestry

It is recorded that 82% of Romani people were born in England. While the Romani people are discriminated against everywhere, there are quite a number of Romani celebrities in many fields. That includes Charlie Chaplin, the great actor and creator of Modern Arts; Pablo Picasso; Elvis Presley, the US celebrity singer; and Yul Brunner and Michael Cain, the great Hollywood actors who also had Romani ancestry.

Flamenco, the famous Spanish dance form, is believed to have roots in the Romani dance and was introduced to Spain by them.

THINK SMALL: FROM PEOPLE'S OWN IN GERMANY TO AMERICA'S DARLING! GOLIATH WON HERE, TOO

It is said that the Creator must have had an inordinate fondness for Beetles, as there are more than 400,000 known species of them. But one Beetle was unique. Here I am writing about this Beetle, which is idiosyncratic in design and size but created history in the automobile industry for being on the production line for 65 years - from 1938 to 2003! The VW Beetle. The French called it 'Lady Bug'. Indonesians named it a 'Frog'. The Bolivians named it a 'Turtle'. There were a few more names like 'the Flea' and 'the Mouse'. But in 1938, the New York Times called it the 'Beetle', and the name caught on like wildfire!

The original design is from 1920 by none other than Ferdinand Porsche and 2 specialists hired by him. Later, Hitler, in Feb 1938, showcased the prototype of this small, inexpensive, bug-shaped family car, which he wanted to be a 'People's car' -Volkswagen- in German. It did, years later, but not the way Hitler envisaged. Hitler thought that such a car and Autobahns could be used as political tools for Germany's rise as a world power. It was put into production by the British after the WW2.

Finally, when it arrived in American markets, the car was shoved off by the public and professionals alike. 'Too ugly and too noisy' was the general comment. Detroit, the American automobile hub, was too busy to even acknowledge the arrival of just 2 Beetles in 1949! But as the car manufacturer hired the Manhattan Ad agency DDB, the fight was like between David and Goliath. Goliath was Detroit, the VW Beetle was David, while DDB's creativity was the sling. David won here, too. 'Think small' was the most famous ad for the VW Beetle. It so happened that it is even considered one of the best of the 20th century. And I can assure you that this article is not just limited to a car nut but fuses with industry, business and history not well-known to many of us.

Touch of Porsche and Hitler

Bela Barenyi from Austria-Hungary, who was adjudged to be the Car Engineer of the Century in 1999, is credited with the original design of the Beetle. Along with him, another Austrian automobile engineer, Erwin Komenda, whose services were hired by Ferdinand Porsche, founder of the great brand, came up with the design of this small car as early as the early 1920s. Porsche later became a Nazi party member of Hitler. In Feb 1938, none other than Hitler showcased the prototype of a small, inexpensive dream car which was intended to be owned by any German family at the Berlin Auto Show. That was the first and last show of Beetle under that regime, and only about 600 cars were produced by the company, which was named Volkswagen (VW) in German, meaning 'People's car'. But it didn't take-off further as WW2 broke out, and thereafter, VW was busy with building warfare machines using free slave labour.

Here I think I have to mention another name among the pioneer team of Ferdinand Porsche, whose name was taken out of records by the Nazis. He was Joseph Ganz, a Jewish automobile engineer.

Resurrection

The main factory of VW at Wolfsburg, Germany, was raided by Allied air forces many times during the war, and the main building itself was in debris. After the war, this factory fell into what became a designated British zone. The British maintained a repair shop in the same factory using the same employees but wanted to dispose of the factory for their own interests at the earliest - like any occupying force, perhaps!

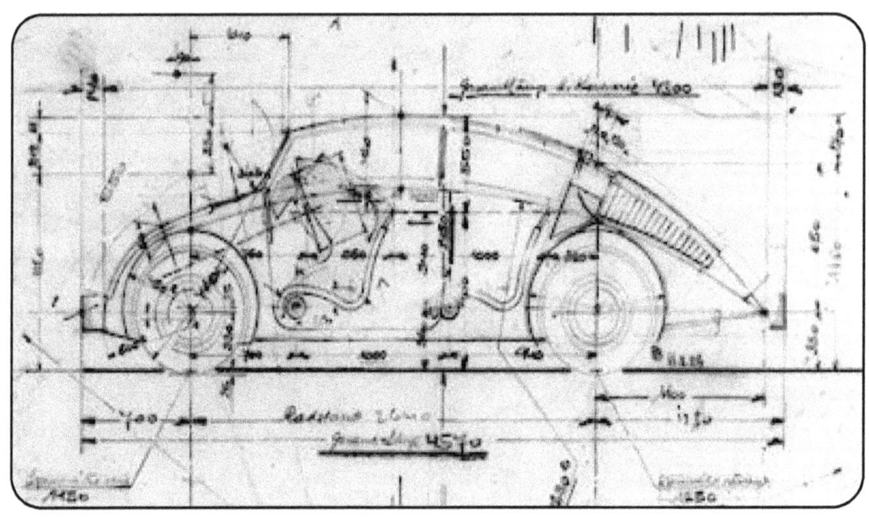

The original design of Beetle done by Bela Barenyi in 1920, perfect!

In March 1948, a delegation, including Henry Ford II, travelled to Germany to negotiate a proposal to take over the VW car factory by the invitation of the British. But for some reason, it didn't click. Many other moves for the sell-off didn't work out either. Finally, the British gave control of the Wolfsburg factory to the German state under a former GM, Heinz Nordhoff. He restarted the production line in earnest, though slowly. By 1948, about 2,154 cars per month started flowing out. In the same year, Beetles started exports as well.

During the 1950s, Beetle sales skyrocketed. While keeping the same shape of the body, technical features were upgraded or replaced constantly. By July 1953, the 500,000th car rolled out of the assembly line and in another 2 years, in 1955, 1 millionth.

Beetle Hit the American Automobile Market

The popularity of the Beetle swelled in the 1960s in America. Carl Hahn of VW signed an agreement in 1956 with the American ad firm DDB Doyle Dane Bernbach- which goes strong to this date worldwide with a revenue of more than $2.4 billion in 2012- and paid $ 600,000. Though this amount was too big for VW, it was a time when brands like Chevrolet and Ford each were spending $ 30 million a year for their ad campaigns.

At a time when Americans loved cars made in Detroit, how could the DDB sell such a small, inexpensive, probably ugly-to-look-at-a-glance foreign car that Hitler had a hand in creating for the Americans? It was a challenge. Americans dreamed of cars of big size and expensive features! Like a Biblical David (Beetle) against Goliath (Detroit) situation! But here, too, history says that David finally won against Goliath.

DDB came out with many ads with different titles featuring Beetle's specialities. But 'Think Small', which was created in 1959, did the magic. This is even considered the best ad campaign of the ad industry in the 20th century! Helmut Krone and Julian Norman Koenig of DDB created it. VW exported 423,000 Beetle cars to the US in 1968 alone! Thanks to this advertisement, many Americans bought a Beetle as their first car out of college or a second car for the family.

It was not a surprise that VW Beetle was featured by Walt Disney in 1969 as 'Herbie', which was a hit movie. Thereafter, another 5 movies were released worldwide till 2005. So also numerous American TV serials. I think even now, those films are popular on OTT platforms.

Down goes the sales, and finally out

By the 1970s, competition for the Beetle came from Honda's Civic and other Japanese brands, even from VW's own Golf! Less petrol consumption, more space for passengers, and lower costs were challenges raised by them and others. A weak US dollar at that time was another reason. Finally, by 1977, stricter American standards for emissions sealed the fate of the Beetle in the US! By that time, around 5 million cars had been sold in the US alone. Total sales of this model were about 23 million in the world. The last car rolled out from their factory in Mexico on July 21, 2003!

"It's ugly, but it gets you there" was another hit ad campaign by VW Beetle. They did that for 65 years consecutively.

THIS APPLE IN THE HAND KEEPS ME AWAKE

It was in 1665 that Isaac Newton formulated his great gravitational theory after watching an apple fall straight down rather than sideways or even upward. The impact of his findings remains one of the most popular scientific achievements to date.

Much later, in 1976, 2 college dropouts decided to use the same apple as the name and logo of their company. Their intention was to make small computers that are user-friendly for people. The Apple Computer Company so, formed by Steve Jobs and Steve Wozniak- there was a third cofounder also named Ronald Wayne who left the company after 2 weeks- may be valued at more than 2 trillion US dollars or more as of now! Hundreds of millions of people use Apple products every day worldwide- iBook, iPod, iPhone, iPad, and Apple Watch are some of them. As known today, Apple Inc. sells through their Apple stores while miles of queues of people emerge in front of them in each town when new products are introduced! Now, India has opened multiple Apple stores, producing iPhones and expects that in another 5 years, more than half of Apple products in the world will be produced from India- making a shift from China.

Here, I am covering the story of the transformation of their first logo, which showed Sir Isaac Newton and his apple to what it is today- an apple with a byte, oops, and a bite. Read about Apple Computers, which you don't know, though you may be

using their products for years, including the truth that Steve Jobs was fired by his own company once!

Coloured version of the first logo

The Beginning: Why Did They Choose an Apple?

Founded on April 1, 1976, Apple Computers started operations in Steve Jobs' garage. Their first product, Apple I, was sold without a monitor the same year. Next year, in 1977, they added the monitors. Within 4 years of existence, they could make sales of 117 million when they decided to go public in 1980.

Steve Jobs was a vegetarian, a fruitarian, to be exact. He was an environmentalist also. He had spent some time in India as well to experience Zen Buddhism. Jobs worked as a video game designer with a US firm named Atari, which was founded in

1972. When he named the firm Apple, Jobs could have had the intention of listing in the phonebook ahead of Atari! This could be the logical reason why he and his partners chose an apple to name their company.

In 1974, Jobs reconnected with his high school friend Stephen Wozniak, who was with Hewlett Packard Co. They had a third partner named Ronald Wayne, who designed their first logo with Sir Isaac Newton sitting under an apple tree with a ripened apple looming large about to fall! Strangely, within 12 days of existence, Ronald Wayne left the organisation and later sold his 10% share of $800 to his partners!

Evolution of Logos

In 1977, one year after the first logo depicting the apple about to fall on the head of Sir Isaac Newton, with the caption 'Newton: A mind forever voyaging through strange seas of thought alone', they decided to change drastically. This time, they went for an apple in rainbow colours. The designer went to include a bite on the apple to differentiate it from that of a cherry! The apple with a bite continues to remain as their logo, despite the fact that they have changed the colours and shades from time to time.

How was Steve Jobs Fired from His Own Company?

Strange things can happen in the corporate world, as I know firsthand! As Apple Inc. was getting established and professionally growing, the 2 cofounders thought that they should have a CEO who was senior to them and mature enough to guide the company to greater heights. When Steve Jobs zeroed in on John Sculley, the CEO of Pepsico, the latter was not interested in joining them. "Do you want to sell sugar water for the rest of your life, or do you want to come with me and change the world?" Jobs is recorded to have asked Sculley. However, Sculley joined Apple Inc. in 1983.

Two years later, over 2 new products launched -the Lisa and the Macintosh- as they failed to perform in sales returns, Jobs and Sculley had to quarrel. The issue was taken to the board. In 1985, the board decided to fire Steve Jobs, leaving Apple without the input of the iconic founder!

It took another 12 years as Apple company confronted more and more problems without a stalwart like Jobs; the board decided to call back the services of Steve Jobs in 1997! I am not going to elaborate on what Steve Jobs did here. The world would not have been the same without his contribution!

UNBUTTONING THE PAST: AND KOUMPOUNOPHOBIA

Buttons are so common in our everyday life. Yet I have chosen to write an article about it mainly because it is only recently that I came to know that buttons were invented by ancient Indians apart from the fact that a lot of unknown history is behind them. Buttons are actually much more ancient than what most of us believe. It starts with the fact that buttons were invented by the Indus Valley Civilisation of ancient India, which dates back to 3000 BC! Initially, they were used for decorative and ornamental purposes than fasteners.

But it took a long time before the first button and buttonhole closure systems, as we use them now, were invented by the Germans in the 13th century!

Buttons come mostly in round shapes but are different in materials and colours! It started with sea shells at Mohenjo Daro and then moved to bones, horn, metal, Ivory, rubber, ceramic, glass and plastic (cellulose). Let us go through the chronological history of buttons.

Indus (Sindhu) valley civilisation

Sindhu Valley civilisation is one of the earliest civilisations, comparable to those of Egypt and Mesopotamia. Currently located in India and Pakistan, it is a marvel of ancient times with well-planned cities, streets, drainage systems and great public baths. The name is so derived from the river names Sindhu (Indus was the name given by the British who invented this). It is also known as the Sindhu-Saraswati civilisation, which was named after an ancient river that has become extinct now.

The first button is confirmed to have originated there about 5000 years ago. Made out of a curved shell at Mohenjo Daro, it was used for ornamental purposes to exhibit the status of the person who wore it and was used individually.

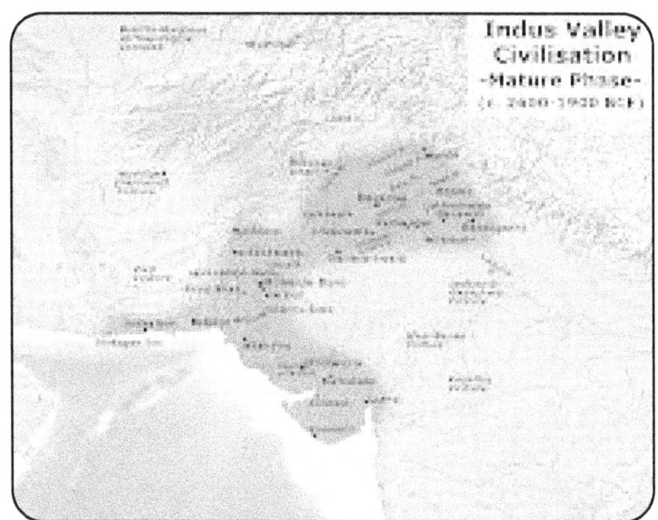

Further

It is recorded that buttons were used in Scotland from 2200 to 1800 BC and in China during the Bronze Age from 2000 to 1500 BC. Buttons were used by ancient Romans and Greeks as well.

It was in the Middle Ages that buttons were used as fasteners. However, only those who were rich were allowed to wear a lot of buttons on dresses. The Industrial Revolution popularised the use of buttons among the masses. Mathew Boulton, an English manufacturer, introduced costly cut steel buttons in the middle of the 18th century.

How Do You Size Up a Button?

A measuring system known as 'Lignes' is used to size up the button- 40 lines are 1 inch. It is abbreviated by the letter 'L'. The ligne had originated in France prior to the use of the Metric system- which was a byproduct of the French Revolution- in the 18th century. It is still used in France and Switzerland among watchmakers and button makers!

Koumpounophobia

There is a phobia related to buttons, especially for the bad, smelly, and dirty buttons. About 1% of Americans are identified with this phobia! The late Steve Jobs, cofounder of Apple Inc., had suffered from this phobia. It is recorded.

WHAT THE LITTLE BOY AND FAT MAN DID TO THE WORLD

The recent release of the Hollywood movie Oppenheimer, brought to my mind an avalanche of related thoughts, not mentioned in the movie, about the dropping of the first atomic bomb. I was not born then. The 'Little Boy'- Thin Man was the original name- and the 'Fat Man' were the names given to the atomic bombs by the Americans which were used in Japan. Why did the Americans give those funny names- which don't look funny to me- anyway?

The American bomber aircraft which dropped the bomb at Hiroshima was named 'Enola Gay'. But who gave this strange name to this bomber? The pilot did. His name was Paul Tibbitts. He chose the name to honour his own old mother! Finally, was it an honour or dishonour for her, I don't know. Paul, who thought himself to be a hero to his countrymen, finally decided not to have an engraved grave, fearing backlash from protestors for years to come.

On August 6, 1945, the 'Little Boy' was dropped over Hiroshima! Three days later, on August 9, the 'Fat Man' was dropped over Nagasaki! The world was never the same again. In fact, Nagasaki was not the original primary target; it was another city named Kokura. But on that fateful day, Kokura was in morning fog! As such, the pilot mistakenly or otherwise targeted secondary Nagasaki- which culminated in a new expression, 'Kokura's luck.'

I hope this article will enthuse youngsters, especially the new generation, on the subject. Many oldies of my generation as well may not be aware of these historical facts; many of them were classified information once. For example, America decided not to include Albert Einstein, one of the greatest Physicists, to chair or even in the team 'Manhattan Project' formed to build the first atomic bomb. America decided to drop atomic bombs on Japan in spite of it being explicitly clear that Germany didn't have one, as they surrendered unconditionally. Why?

Models of Fat Man and Little Boy on display at the Bradbury Science Museum Los Alamos National Laboratory. Image courtesy of Los Alamos National Laboratory.

From Pupil Hall, Manhattan to Los Alamos Desert, New Mexico Desert

On atomic theory, a forerunner of making such a bomb, a number of scientists have contributed. Among them, John Dalton and Frederick Sodely, both English scientists of the 18th century, and Pierre and Marie Currie, French scientists and Rutherford, the New Zealand scientists of the early 19th century, stand out. There could be others. Interestingly, HG Wells, an English scientific fiction writer, wrote about an atomic bomb as early as 1914 in his novel 'The World Set Free'. There were efforts to split the atoms among France, Italy, Japan and Germany from the late 19th and 20th centuries.

As the Nazis came to power in Germany in 1933, many leading Jewish scientists fled from that country for safe havens. In spite of this exodus, German Scientists Hahn and Strassmann could lead an operation there to make an atomic bomb. Leo Szilard, a leading German scientist, came to the US and joined the University of Chicago in 1942 and joined efforts to make the bomb. Prior to that, in 1939, scientists at Columbia University could successfully conduct a nuclear fission experiment in the basement of a physics lab named Pupil Hall, right in the heart of Manhattan, very close to Broadway! Hardly anyone knew that then, even in the US!

In August 1939, Albert Einstein wrote an official letter drafted by Szilard to then US President Franklin D Roosevelt warning of the impending danger of the Germans if successful in making an atomic bomb. Though the US made serious efforts only after they entered WWII, a committee was formed which eventually gave birth to the secret move named Manhattan Project' to make a bomb in 1942! Leslie Groves, an officer from the US Corps of Engineers, headed it, while the team of scientists was headed by Robert Oppenheimer, another German Jew who migrated to America. Interestingly, Albert Einstein was sidelined by the Govt since he was thought to be left-leaning politically, and US Army intelligence didn't clear his name. He was listed as a security risk. However, on July 16, 1945, in the desert named Los Alamos near New Mexico, US, the first nuclear test took place, codenamed 'Trinity'! Robert Oppenheimer, father of the nuclear bomb, didn't live long as a hero there!

From Los Alamos Desert to Hiroshima and Nagasaki

Harry Truman came to the seat of Presidentship in the US soon after the death of President Roosevelt on April 12, 1945. Team Manhattan was ready with bombs as they recommended a short list of cities in Japan, including Hiroshima and Kokura, to be bombed as primary targets. They selected the cities least affected by bombing thus far so that the effects of the bombs could be measured better and the world could possibly see the might of a new military power on earth!

Meanwhile, it was known that Germany was no longer a nuclear threat as the country surrendered to the Allied forces on May 7, 1945. As such, 2 petitions signed by Leo Szilard and 59 other scientists involved, including Robert Oppenheimer, in making the atomic bombs urged the US President, commander-in-chief, in July 1945, not to use the atomic bomb in Japan. Unfortunately, such petitions never reached the President as Leslie Gores, Head of the military, sat on it.

Both bombs were transported to Tinian Island, Japan, which was under the command of American forces on the ship USS 'Indianapolis' for assembly on July 26, 1945. Four days later, this very ship was torpedoed by the Japanese forces, another hardly known part of history! On August 6, 1945, at 2.00 AM, the American Bomber B29 Superfortress named Enola Gay left the Japanese isle of Tinian and headed for Hiroshima. At 08.15 AM local time, the 'Little Boy' exploded! Three days later, on August 9, the second bomber, named 'Bock's Car', dropped the 'Fat Man' over Nagasaki at 11.02 AM local time! The name of the second bomber was so given by the pilot Frederick Bock, who was selected to drop the Fat Man at Nagasaki. But on that fateful day, due to technical reasons, another pilot, Charles Tweeny, did that, which could be another twist in history!

TAILPIECE

Enola Gay is 'proudly' exhibited at the National Air and Space Museum in Washington, DC, while Bock's Car is on display at the US Air Force Museum in Ohio. I have seen Enola Gay in full sheen, which is displayed in Washington, but I could not appreciate it for some reason. But the meaningful funeral silence maintained by the visitors at Peace Memorial in Hiroshima, which I experienced 6 years back, lingers in my mind to this day!

Before I conclude this article, I also have to mention the Indian connection of Robert Oppenheimer. He was a German Jew by birth, but like many other German scientists and philosophers, he was interested in Indian Hindu scriptures, especially 'Bhagavad Gita'. After his initial interest in the book reading the translated version, he took all the pains to study Sanskrit, the original language in which the book was written thousands of years back, to know more in-depth about the meaning of the verses in the book first-hand.

WRESTLING, WHISKEY AND OVAL OFFICE? IT'S BETTER THAN YOU WOULD BELIEVE

Do you know that 13 of the US presidents were professional wrestlers before they came to the White House? Incredible but true. I do not know whether there is something special between wrestling and American Presidentships. But some of the most successful at the Oval Office - including George Washington and Abraham Lincoln- were wrestlers who were enlisted in the National Hall of Fame.

When George Washington was chosen as the first President of America to the new position, it could have been just a chance that a wrestler happened to reach that position, despite the fact that he was a champ in the field and used to wrestle until he came to that position. But what about others? Can Hulk Hogan ever come to the Oval Office? I will not be surprised if he does, since so many Hollywood stars also could make it as President or senator influencing affairs of the world.

Do you know that George Washington was a businessman who also had a distillery that was the largest in the US at that time? He set up a distillery producing 11000 gallons of whiskey after his term as President was over! It could be the fact since I am an Indian that these true stories of American Presidents are a bit shocking to me. Anyway, I would like to share what I have learned from American history.

WWE

Wrestling is originally the oldest of all sports and has been depicted even in cave paintings dating back 15000 years. The ancient Greeks were prolific wrestlers. As they created the Olympic Games in the 8th century BC, wrestling was featured in the event. In the US, the English in the colonies and the French in Canada made wrestling a popular sport at their social gatherings.

In the US, one of the earliest sports was wrestling. When the Europeans arrived there, wrestling was already an established sport with Native Americans in the 15th and 16th centuries. Sure, the intention of Native Americans could have been to become skilled warriors, and their styles went from tribe to tribe. This trend was also transferred among the colonists.

The World Wrestling Entertainment (WWE) is the biggest professional wrestling company based in the USA. To the best of my understanding, WWE shows are all cooked up and scripted. Once I knew this fact, I myself lost interest in such shows that used to be telecast years back. However, it is a money-spinning event to this day with a lot of admirers and followers.

Having been exposed to WWE years back did not bring my observations to the fact that a lot of American Presidents were once professional wrestlers. I learned this info while reading a detailed biography of Abraham Lincoln!

The Wrestler Presidents

1. John Adams.
2. Chester A Arthur.
3. Calvin Coolidge.
4. D. Eisenhower.
5. James Garfield.
6. Ulysses S Grant.
7. Andrew Jackson.
8. Abraham Lincoln.
9. Franklin Pierce.
10. Theodore Roosevelt.
11. William H Taft.
12. Zachary Taylor.
13. George Washington.

George Washington was one of the country's first wrestling champions at the age of 18. He continued wrestling almost till he became the first US president!

First and Only Distilling President

I read about the honesty of George Washington in my younger days. While he was a boy of old, with an axe he received as a gift, he cut a cherry tree which was nursed dearly by his father in the garden. Later, when his father found that out, young George was bold enough to tell the truth, which was appreciated by his father! Now, I find this story reported as a myth in many journals, including Encyclopedia Britannica. Whether to believe Britannica or not, like BBC itself, is a different matter, though!

George Washington started making whisky commercially in 1797 with his 2250 sq. ft distillery, the largest in the country at that time. They produced 11000 gallons of whiskey at Mount Vernon. His employees also included a few black slaves!

Since 2007, US Govt has recreated a similar facility of 1787 at the same location, and it is a tourist attraction!

GANDHI? WHO'S THAT?

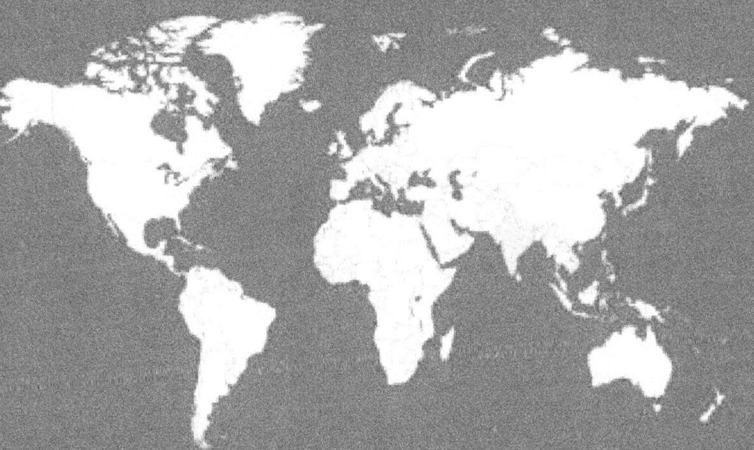

Though nominated five times, how and why the
Nobel foundation ignored him! And
64 other hardly known but should know articles

JAISON CHACKO

KALEIDOSCOPIC MUSINGS
JAISON CHACKO